The Italian Family Kitchen

The Italian Family Kitchen

Authentic Recipes That Celebrate Italian Homestyle Cooking

Eva Santaguida & Harper Alexander

Creators of Pasta Grammar

ROCK
POINT

Rock Point titles are also available at discount for retail, wholesale,
promotional and bulk purchase. For details, contact the Special
Sales Manager by email at specialsales@quarto.com or by mail at
The Quarto Group, Attn: Special Sales Manager, 100 Cummings
Center Suite, 265D, Beverly, MA 01915, USA.

10 9 8 7 6 5 4 3

ISBN: 978-1-57715-432-7

Digital edition published in 2024
eISBN: 978-0-7603-8896-9

Library of Congress Control Number: 2024934807

Publisher: Rage Kindelsperger
Creative Director: Laura Drew
Editorial Director: Erin Canning
Managing Editor: Cara Donaldson
Cover Design: Laura Klynstra
Book Layout: Danielle Smith-Boldt
Food Photography: Elysa Weitala, all except the following pages:
4, 15, 17, 18, 21, 25, 26, 36-37, 72, 94, 97, 110, 123, 128
Additional Photography: Eva Santaguida & Harper Alexander: 14, 15, 17,
18, 21, 23, 25, 26, 36-37, 122; Getty Images: Shaun Egan (back cover)
Food Styling: Victoria Woollard, all except the following pages: 69, 72, 91,
94, 97, 110, 123, 128
Food Stylist Assistants: Allee Cakmis & Francesca Sossi

Printed in China

To our parents,
✣ who taught us ✣
that food is love.

⊰ CONTENTS ⊱

⊰ INTRODUCTION ⊱

People often ask us why our YouTube channel is called "Pasta Grammar." The name came from a revelation (on my part, Eva already knew in her bones what I was to discover) that arose out of a lighthearted argument during our wedding feast.

The debate began when my American family was politely informed by Eva's Italian family that spaghetti and meatballs do not belong on the same plate. They were taken aback and became defensive of their beloved dish. This prompted Eva to launch into a full-blown lesson on the "rules" of pasta: which sauces belong with which pasta shapes, what ingredients pair well, and when certain exceptions to these strict requirements are permitted.

Up until our marriage, Eva had worked as an Italian language teacher. She even had her own school in Umbria. During that feast, I saw her addressing the table like she was in her classroom, and that's when it hit me: Italian food is a language.

The Italian menu and cooking approach has systems and "rules" that resemble grammar and syntax. Like all grammatical systems, there are exceptions to every rule. Often, to a non-native, these rules and exceptions can seem nonsensical. On the other hand, someone who is fluent in the language would be baffled by their own perception of nonsense if the rules are ignored.

The Italian insistence on strictly adhering to the grammar of their food has led to a lot of criticism and skepticism. *Who cares? If I like spaghetti and meatballs, what's the big deal?*

Here there seems to be a fundamental misunderstanding. While almost all Italians certainly think that pineapple on pizza is unappetizing (to use a polite word), the issue is rarely that anyone in Italy cares what someone else enjoys eating in their own kitchen. Instead, they are merely expressing that certain combinations of ingredients do not fit into the framework of Italian culinary grammar. It may taste good to you, but it's definitely not Italian food.

Beyond the grammatical similarity, Italian food is inextricably tied to language, in that Italians spend a lot more time talking about food than they do eating it. Every conversation inevitably turns to cuisine as they recount the stories behind the food they cook. One of the most amusing aspects of adjusting to life in an Italian family was getting used to spending an entire meal talking about and planning for the *next* meal. Everyone chimes in, giving their two cents about how the proposed dishes were born, the best way to make them, the right season to eat them in, and which Italian region makes the best version. Most importantly, they reminisce about memories the recipe brings to mind and fondly praise the people they've shared it with.

Perhaps the truest and most fundamental philosophy of Italian food is that the stories make the recipes taste better. Maybe you can cook a decent ragù in an Instant Pot in 15 minutes. And, maybe, in a blind taste test, even Eva couldn't tell the difference. But food is not experienced in a vacuum, and you'll miss out on a lot of storytelling over a simmering, aromatic pot. Food is more than the correct blend of flavor and nutrients to satisfy our lizard brains. It is an all-encompassing expression of everything that's most important in life: health, peace, compassion, love, friendship, community, spirituality, and family.

On our YouTube channel, to the best of our abilities, we mirror this philosophy not just by sharing recipes but also by telling the stories behind the dishes. These stories continue to evolve, and there's always room for more. Possibilities and innovations abound in Italian cuisine, but before you can write poetry, you must first learn the grammar. This book is an introduction to the basic language of Italian cuisine so that readers can gain the tools necessary for creating their own Italian food stories.

It's difficult to sum up Italian food in a single volume, but in the following pages, you will find a collection of recipes from all over Italy, representing some of the best food the country has to offer. Every recipe is written, to the best of our abilities, according to the grammar of Italian cuisine. In a world where too many Italian dishes are "translated" to suit the perceived differences of foreign tastes, we're proud to offer the real food of Italy as it is cooked and eaten by Italian home cooks today.

THE ITALIAN MENU EXPLAINED

The Italian menu consists of five courses: antipasti, primi, secondi, contorni, and dolci. This can cause some confusion when foreigners visit Italian restaurants and are unsure what to order. The confusion can be compounded by the addition of a few extra snacks served in between. Here, we briefly explain each course and how they are served.

Pane

Pane, or bread, is not a course in and of itself, but it is a mandatory element, and its presence is required as long as savory food is being served. Not only is it eaten by itself, but it is also used to mop up extra sauce left on the plate. This practice is called the "scarpetta," and there is no better compliment given to the chef. Bread is a must on every Italian table.

Antipasto

This course is pretty simple to grasp, as it roughly corresponds to what many of us would consider to be an appetizer. An antipasto is often just an assortment of snacking ingredients, rather than a prepared dish. For example, you may encounter a variety of cheeses, salame, cold cuts, or simple bruschette. Sometimes antipasti can be small, fried treats, such as Crocchette di Riso (page 42). In short, antipasti are small snacks served before the main courses. With a few exceptions, such as a caprese (which is really just cheese, anyway), salads are never served as an antipasto.

Primo

A primo, or first course, is a carb-based main. In other words, primi are generally pasta or risotto dishes. Traditionally, a primo is followed by a secondo, but this doesn't have to be the

case. It's perfectly acceptable to choose one or the other as a main course. What is unacceptable on an Italian table is serving a primo with a secondo or a contorno on the same plate. Nothing makes an Italian cringe quite like seeing pasta and a salad served together. There are a few notable exceptions, such as Risotto alla Milanese (page 129), which is served with Ossobuco alla Milanese (page 147), but in general, you will always see a primo served by itself.

Secondo

A secondo, or second course, is usually a meat or fish dish. Once again, while it traditionally follows a primo you can certainly skip the first course entirely. There are some dishes, such as Parmigiana di Melanzane (page 144), that can fall into the secondo category despite being vegetarian.

Contorno

A contorno is a vegetable-based side dish, often served with (or at the same time as) a secondo.

Frutta

This one can really trip up guests at an Italian family feast. After a huge assortment of antipasti, which seemed like a full meal, followed by a pasta or rice dish, followed by an unexpected meat or fish secondo, a few bowls or plates of fresh fruit come out of the kitchen and everyone digs in. *Ah, the guest thinks, a nice, light dessert to finish things off.* This is just the warm-up, which leads to the . . .

Dolce

This is the simplest course of all that requires no explanation. Dessert.

THE ITALIAN PANTRY

While we won't cover every ingredient you're likely to need for Italian home cooking, here is a list of some key pantry staples that require some explanation and tips on how to source them.

Extra-Virgin Olive Oil (EVOO)

Olive oil comes in a few different grades of quality, but the only one worth considering for any edible purpose is extra virgin, a term that signifies an acceptably low acidity. The olive oil business is full of marketing trickery, so it's important to carefully read the fine print of the bottle to discover where it was made, when it was harvested, and how it has been treated. Olive oil does go bad, so, if possible, try to avoid a harvest date of more than a year before the purchase date (most manufacturers don't include this information, of course). Be aware that many olive-oil companies label their bottles in mischievous ways that make it seem like the oil is Italian, but that's not always the case. Most bottles include some fine print with a code that lists the actual countries of origin (IT = Italy, ES = Spain, TN = Tunisia, GR = Greece, etc.). Not that olive oil from these countries is bad; it's just nice to avoid imported Italian prices on olive oil that was made in Tunisia for a fraction of the cost. Ultimately, what's most important is that the oil tastes good to you, so don't be afraid to try a few different kinds and see what you like most.

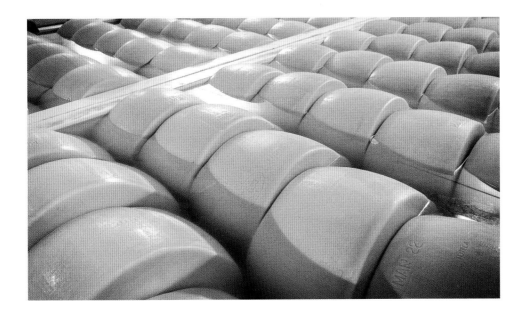

Lard

Despite popular conception, the use of olive oil in Italian cooking is a shockingly recent phenomenon. Modern technology has made oil very delicious, but that wasn't always the case. In days past, olive oil was used to light lamps, whereas the cooking fat of choice (particularly in the south) was pork lard. Even today, the presence of lard in a recipe is a key indicator that the dish in question is an old tradition with a lot of history. The only thing we need to add is a plea to not fear lard, which has been unfairly demonized. While it's certainly not a "health" food, it's better for you than butter.

Parmigiano-Reggiano Cheese

The king of Italian cheeses, Parmigiano-Reggiano is the most popular cheese for seasoning and topping food in Italy. It is absolutely not the same thing as Parmesan, which should be avoided like the plague. Luckily, the real deal is widely available and easy to distinguish. By law, any cheese that is sold as "Parmigiano-Reggiano" (and stamped with this name on the rind) is genuine. There is another cheese, Grana Padano, that is very similar and used in Italy as a more economical substitute. You can use Grana if you like, although, ironically, we've found it to be more expensive and harder to find outside of Italy than the superior Parmigiano.

Pecorino Cheese

Pecorino simply means "sheep cheese," and there are many different kinds. It's sharper and saltier than cow cheese and a staple in many boldly flavored Italian dishes. Outside of Italy, the most common variety is pecorino Romano. We've chosen to refer to it throughout the book simply as "pecorino," because any aged pecorino (meaning it's hard and can be grated) will work in the recipes.

Mozzarella Cheese

The best mozzarella comes floating in milky water. In general, try to stay away from low-moisture cheese. It can be frustrating trying to find really good mozzarella outside of Italy, so many are tempted to try to make it at home. Just be aware that all the simple recipes you're likely to find do not make real mozzarella, which requires a more complicated culture process.

Ricotta

We have searched high and low in the United States for even a spoonful of real ricotta, without any luck whatsoever (even at Italian markets that make it in-house). Even more so than mozzarella, the homemade recipes that are bandied about have nothing to do with ricotta. Ricotta isn't really a cheese; it's made by re-cooking (ri-cotta, get it?) the leftover whey from a previous cheesemaking process. Little bits of protein solidify and float to the top: that's ricotta. The real stuff is quite lean, unlike the fake copies found in grocery stores, which are too fatty and creamy. The two have totally different tastes and textures. While we sometimes make our own ricotta at home, using the traditional process, it can be challenging for many who don't have access to fresh, raw milk. Find the best you can and don't shy away from the skim-milk versions, which are often closer to the real thing.

Guanciale

Guanciale is cured pork jowl. It should be very firm, dark, and have a peppery crust (which should always be trimmed off). Due to the growing popularity of authentic Pasta alla Carbonara (page 116), it's luckily becoming more widely available online and in specialty stores. We've seen some horrible imitations, though, so please stay away from anything that looks soft and spongy.

Prosciutto

The major thing to note here is the difference between prosciutto crudo (raw prosciutto) and prosciutto cotto (cooked prosciutto). The former is cured pork leg, the cold cut that most of us associate with prosciutto. The latter is cooked pork leg, or ham. For prosciutto crudo cooking purposes, seek out prosciutto di Parma or prosciutto di San Daniele, which are on the sweeter side. Other prosciutto crudo versions can be much saltier and are more suited to an antipasto plate.

Sausages

Most sausages in Italy are extremely simple, usually made with nothing more than pork, salt, and black pepper. While you can use the sausage of your choice, we generally advise staying away from anything that is heavily spiced, flavored, or seasoned. You can always season the dish as you like, so it's better to start with neutral meat.

Tuna

Canned tuna has a bad rap in the United States, but when made properly, it is high quality and delicious. Italian tuna comes in cans or jars (the latter is preferable because you can see the quality before buying) and is made with whole chunks of tuna stored in olive oil. Although it's sometimes pricey, we've found great options online and in Mediterranean markets.

All-Purpose or "00" Flour

The term "all purpose" refers to a specific protein content in the flour, whereas "00" signifies a particular fineness of grind in Italy. While they're not the same, they're generally interchangeable for most simple recipes, such as fresh egg pasta (page 22). The recipes will denote any cases where one can't be substituted for the other.

Semolina Flour

Semolina flour is coarsely ground durum wheat. It's very common in southern Italy and gives a much more rustic feel to bread and pasta. This is the kind of flour used to make dry pasta, such as spaghetti and rigatoni. It's also great for dusting dough when you don't want the flour to be absorbed, such as when making pizza dough (page 67).

Bread Flour

There are many cases in Italian cuisine where a very high-protein or high-gluten flour is needed (such as Pizza alla Napoletana on page 70). While it's not always perfect, bread flour has a much higher protein content than all-purpose flour and is therefore often a good substitute in a pinch.

Bread Crumbs

Bread crumbs are used throughout Italian cuisine, from thickening and coating to making a crispy topping for pasta. If you buy your bread crumbs, carefully check the ingredients and look for the simplest version possible. Avoid flavorings and ingredients you can't pronounce. Usually, bread crumbs are dry and crunchy, but there are some instances when fresh bread crumbs are needed (such as in Polpette al Sugo on page 149). Fresh bread crumbs can be made by simply grating or blending a loaf of bread that is a day or two old. To make dried bread crumbs, cut a loaf of bread into small squares, spread them on a baking sheet, and bake at 300ºF (150ºC) until hard and crunchy. Chop them up in a blender or food processor until you achieve the fineness of grind you prefer.

Rice

There are many different rice varieties in Italy, but the most common are arborio, carnaroli, and vialone nano. They are very different from Asian rice and perfect for thick, starchy dishes such as risotto. In general, these three types are interchangeable, although in some cases (noted in the recipes), one is more suitable than the others.

Canned Tomatoes and Tomato Passata

If possible, we recommend avoiding store-bought tomato passata or puree and sticking to canned whole peeled tomatoes. The latter can easily be converted into the former by using a vegetable mill, and the quality of whole tomatoes will always be higher than premade puree. That being said, in cases where you need puree and don't have the time to mill your own, you can certainly use a good passata. In either case, it's imperative that the ingredients include nothing beyond pure tomatoes (sometimes citric acid is added). Stay away from anything that is flavored or seasoned; it's up to you to make the dish taste how you want. San Marzano tomatoes are famous for good reason, but we find them to be overpriced in the United States and far from a necessity to cook amazing food. Use them (only if certified; otherwise they're fake) if you want the best but don't feel that you need to spend the extra money.

Peperoncino and Chili Peppers

Calabrian peperoncino chili peppers provide the heat in spicy Italian dishes (which are actually quite rare outside of Calabria). They can be hard to find, but in most cases, a cayenne chili pepper will suffice as a substitute for fresh peperoncini. Dried Calabrian pepper flakes and powder are becoming more widely available but can easily be substituted with red chili pepper flakes and cayenne powder.

Oregano

When it's good, oregano has an incredible flavor and aroma. To have the best, search out dried oregano that comes in a long package with the herb still on the branch, a sure sign of quality. It can be sourced online or at Mediterranean markets and is much better than what you will find in a jar. That being said, you can jar it yourself by carefully rubbing the dried herb off the stems.

Capers

"Normal" capers (stored in brine) will work just fine, but if you happen to run into capers stored in salt, give them a shot. All you need to do is rinse the capers and pat them dry with a paper towel prior to cooking.

TOOLS OF THE TRADE

If you step into an Italian kitchen, you'll likely encounter some unfamiliar kitchen tools. Here, we cover a few essential pieces of cooking gear that no Italian can live without and that you may not have in your cupboards.

Nonna Knife

You'll rarely find a fancy chef's knife in an Italian family's kitchen—perhaps not even a single sharp knife. Italian home cooking is built for practicality and convenience, rather than impressive technique or attention to precision. Most traditional Italian cooks chop everything in their hand with a small, cheap, plastic-handled knife. It's barely sharp, only slightly more so than a butter knife, with a serrated edge. The ingredient is held in one hand and the knife is pressed through it and against the thumb using the other hand. It's certainly not a necessity to use a nonna knife, and most people who weren't raised on this technique will find it challenging and slow; however, it's a good skill to practice, because it can come in quite useful when cooking without a proper knife.

Mattarello

The Italian rolling pin, known as a "mattarello," is quite a bit different than a "normal" pin. It has a very narrow diameter and is ideally quite long, about 3 feet (0.9 m). A good mattarello is essentially just a long, smooth stick without any handles or edges. The advantage of this type of rolling pin is that it can be used to roll very large sheets of dough without causing indentations—very useful when making fresh pasta. We've had luck finding suitably simple mattarelli on craft websites, such as Etsy.

Kitchen Tweezers

Imagine a pair of tweezers the size of large tongs. They can delicately place small ingredients on a plate or be used to twirl big portions of pasta onto a ladle for plating. This versatile tool is widely available online, despite being almost unheard of in the United States. They are highly recommended.

Vegetable Mill

A vegetable mill is most often used for making tomato puree out of fresh or canned tomatoes, but it can also be useful for mashing just about anything. Try making mashed potatoes with one and you'll never go back. Try to find a high-quality mill that is comfortable to hold. Trust us; nothing is worse than a cheap mill that springs open unexpectedly or gives you hand cramps.

Dough Board

This is essentially a large, wooden cutting board with a small lip that catches on the edge of a counter or table to prevent slipping. Look for one that's at least 20 inches (50 cm) square. They're not common in the US, but you can find these on Etsy.

Mandoline

Despite the general lack of precision mentioned in regard to the nonna knife, there are times when ingredients need to be sliced razor thin. In such cases, a mandoline is the best and quickest way to do so. A very sharp, adjustable blade is mounted on a board, and an ingredient can be slid over it to create perfectly consistent slices of any thickness. Mandolines are quite commonly found, although many cooks have never invested in one, but we recommend searching one out.

Pasta Pans

The best pans for making pasta sauces (and finishing pastas) are ceramic-lined frying pans. They're light, nonstick, and safer than some other nonstick coatings. The best kind we've found so far are made by Bialetti, the same company that manufactures the classic Moka coffeepots.

Terra-Cotta Cookware

Beans, stews, and ragù are immeasurably improved when cooked in terra-cotta clay pots. Unfortunately, we've found the options in America for such cookware to be very limited and very expensive. In fact, we make regular trips to Mexico to source our own. The best substitute for a terra-cotta pot is a heavy cast-iron pot with a ceramic lining, like a Dutch oven.

Pasta Machine

While we prefer to roll fresh pasta by hand, a pasta machine is a useful tool for rolling large quantities of dough in consistent sheets. More often than not, we use ours for purposes other than pasta, such as making cannoli shells. The standard machine in Italy is the Atlas Marcato 150, which we highly recommend. See How to Use a Pasta Machine on page 26 for more information.

HOW TO MAKE FRESH EGG PASTA

The prevalence of fresh egg pasta on cooking programs and social media has led to a few misconceptions about it. Contrary to popular belief, not all fresh pasta is made with flour and eggs. Egg pasta is just one type of fresh pasta, with the most common alternative being made with semolina flour and water (see How to Make Fresh Semolina Pasta on page 24). Another common but erroneous belief is that fresh egg pasta is inherently "better" than store-bought dry pasta. This is simply not true; most dry pasta is made without egg and is just different, not inferior to fresh egg pasta. They are different kinds of pasta with different uses. That being said, there is a grain of truth in the misconception: homemade is generally better than store-bought. In the case of egg pasta, the DIY mantra is particularly applicable.

Fresh egg pasta dough is most commonly made into ribbon noodles, such as tagliatelle or pappardelle. It's also used to make large pasta sheets for lasagna (page 121), cannelloni (page 112), ravioli (page 105), and so on. It really shines when paired with meaty sauces, such as Ragù alla Bolognese (page 78).

The basic rule of thumb for making egg pasta dough is to use 1 egg and 100 grams of all-purpose flour per serving. Once exceeding 3 or 4 servings, an extra egg is usually added to the formula (i.e., 500 grams of flour plus 6 eggs for 5 servings). This guideline comes with a caveat: no two eggs are exactly the same size, so take these measurements as a starting place that must be adjusted by feel.

The thickness of fresh egg pasta is largely a matter of taste. We like thicker pasta that has a nice, chewy bite to it, but others prefer a thinner pasta; $1/16$ inch (1.5 mm) is a pretty safe bet to please most palates.

DURATION: 1½ hours ◆ YIELD: 4 servings

3⅓ cups (400 g) all-purpose flour, plus more for dusting

5 large eggs

1. On a large work surface, pour the flour into a pile and use your fingers to hollow out the center so that it resembles a volcano. Crack the eggs into the hollow. Using a fork, whisk the eggs and gradually incorporate the surrounding flour. When the mixture has thickened into a paste, begin folding in more of the flour and kneading the developing dough by hand.

2. As you knead the dough, gradually continue to incorporate the remaining flour. (You don't need to add it all; eggs aren't all the same size, so you may need less flour. Simply leave some flour aside if you achieve the right dough texture before it's all kneaded in.) The pasta dough should be fairly firm and springy but soft enough to knead smooth. It should not be sticky; if it is sticky, dust the dough with more flour. Knead the dough until it is smooth and even. Wrap it in plastic wrap and let rest at room temperature for 30 minutes. Cut the rested dough in half and keep one-half wrapped in plastic while you roll out the other portion.

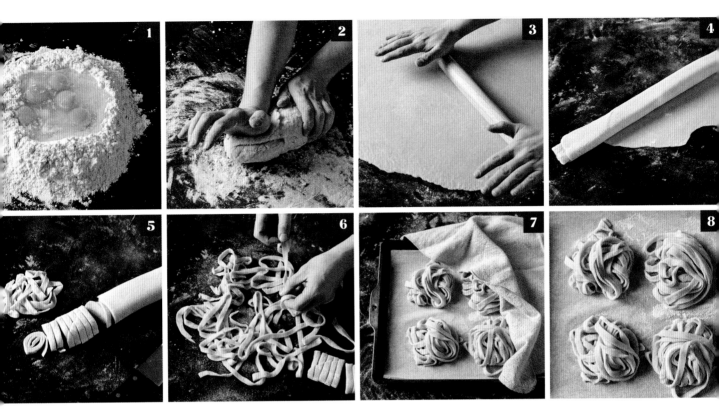

3. On a large, floured work surface, roll out the dough with a rolling pin into a big circle. Flip the sheet over occasionally and dust/rub it frequently with flour on both sides to prevent sticking. Roll it out to a thickness of your liking (or about 1/16 inch, or 1.5 mm), then lightly dust the top with flour.

4. Grasp the edge of the sheet closest to you and fold it forward loosely (the fold should be about 2 inches, or 5 cm, wide). Take this fold and loosely fold it forward again. Continue until the entire sheet is rolled up like a flattened carpet roll.

5. With a sharp knife, cut the flattened roll into slices: for fettuccine (¼ inch, or 6 mm), for tagliatelle (⅓ inch, or 8 mm), or for pappardelle (wider than 1 inch, or 2.5 cm).

6. Gently toss the slices of pasta with your hands to unfold them. If any pieces are stubborn, just unravel them with your fingers.

7. Toss the finished pasta with a generous dusting of flour and arrange it on a baking sheet while you roll out the rest of the dough. (As long as you've dusted the strands with flour, they shouldn't stick together.) Keep the pasta covered with a clean kitchen towel to prevent it from drying out too much.

8. At this point, you can either freeze the pasta for use later or cook it directly (see How to Cook Pasta on page 27). To freeze fresh egg pasta ribbons, arrange the pasta into 4 separate ball-shaped bundles (1 per serving) on a floured platter or baking sheet, then place in the freezer. Once the pasta is frozen solid, transfer the bundles to a plastic bag or other container for more convenient storage. Cook the pasta bundles directly from frozen, but keep in mind that it will take an additional 1 to 2 minutes to boil.

HOW TO MAKE FRESH SEMOLINA PASTA

In southern Italy, fresh pasta isn't made with eggs (see How to Make Fresh Egg Pasta on page 22). Instead, the dough consists simply of semolina flour and water. While this version of fresh pasta is less recognizable around the world, everyone has eaten it in its dry form. That's right; the normal pasta you buy in the store—from spaghetti to farfalle—is made with these same ingredients. The only difference is that fresh pasta is cooked right away, before it has time to dry.

Semolina pasta has a unique advantage over egg pasta in that it is much better suited to forming into interesting shapes. There is a plethora of pasta shapes one can make with semolina pasta dough. One of the easiest is cavatelli. To make it, roll a portion of dough into a snake beneath your palms (keep any pasta you're not working on wrapped in plastic wrap to prevent drying). The snake should be about the width of your pinky finger. Cut this strand into 2-inch (5 cm) pieces. Take a piece, press two fingers into the center, and firmly press and roll the pasta toward you to create a deep depression in the piece of pasta. Cavatelli is excellent with ragù (see Ragù alla Napoletana on page 81).

Another must-try pasta shape is orecchiette, or "little ears." Cut a pinky-width strand into 1-inch (2.5 cm) pieces. Take a piece, press the edge of a butter knife into the center, and firmly roll the knife toward you, almost like you're smearing the piece. The pasta will curl up; unfold it and turn it inside out on your fingertip to create a slightly convex disc. Orecchiette is perhaps best served with broccoli rabe (see Orecchiette alle Cime di Rapa on page 95).

Like for fresh egg pasta, there is a general rule of thumb for measuring the ingredients: 100 grams of semolina flour and 50 ml of water per serving. It's important to recognize that this is only a starting place, as the correct ratio can vary wildly depending on a number of environmental factors. Start with these measurements but be prepared to dust a sticky dough with more flour or to drizzle a dry dough with more water. In the end, you want to achieve a dough that is smooth and consistent (not crumbly) but quite firm and not sticky.

DURATION: 1½ hours ◆ YIELD: 4 servings

3⅓ cups (400 g) semolina flour, plus more for dusting

¾ cup plus 1½ tablespoons (200 ml) water, plus more if needed

1. On a large work surface, pour the flour into a pile and use your fingers to hollow out the center so that it resembles a volcano. Pour the water into the hollow. Using your fingers, stir the water and gradually incorporate the surrounding flour. When the mixture has thickened into a paste, begin folding in more of the flour and kneading the developing dough by hand.

2. As you knead the dough, gradually continue to incorporate the remaining flour. (You don't need to add it all, though; different flours in different conditions absorb varying amounts of water, so you may need less. Simply leave some flour aside if you achieve the right dough texture before it's all kneaded in.) The pasta dough should be firm but soft enough to knead smooth. It should not be sticky; if it does become sticky, dust the dough with more flour. Alternatively, if your pasta dough is too dry and crumbly, drizzle some extra water on top and knead it in.

3. Knead the pasta dough until it is smooth and even. Wrap it in plastic wrap and let rest at room temperature for 30 minutes.

4. Cut off about one-quarter of the dough and keep the remainder wrapped in plastic to prevent it from drying out. Proceed to form this portion into the shape of your choice (see opposite for some suggestions). Generously dust a large baking sheet with flour and arrange the finished pieces there, being careful to keep them from touching. Repeat with the remaining dough, working in batches and keeping unworked dough wrapped in plastic.

5. At this point, you can either freeze the pasta for use later or cook it directly (see How to Cook Pasta on page 27). To freeze fresh pasta, place the baking sheet in the freezer. Once the pasta is frozen solid, transfer it to a plastic bag or other container for more convenient storage. Cook the pasta directly from frozen, but keep in mind that it will take an additional 1 to 2 minutes to boil.

HOW TO USE A PASTA MACHINE

Set up your pasta machine by clamping it to the edge of a counter or table, giving yourself plenty of room to work around it. Dust the machine and the surrounding work surface liberally with flour to avoid sticking. Set the machine to the thickest setting (#0 on a standard Marcato Atlas 150).

It's best to roll sheets of dough in batches, when possible. Cut off a chunk of dough about the size of a tennis ball or smaller. Keep the rest of the dough wrapped in plastic wrap while you work to prevent it from drying out. Flatten the dough ball under your hand until it is about ½ inch (13 mm) thick and dust both sides with flour. Insert one edge of the dough into the wheels of the machine while cranking to draw in the pasta.

Once the pasta emerges from the bottom of the machine, gently pull it out with one hand while continuing to crank it through. Dust the flattened sheet of pasta with flour on both sides, decrease the thickness of the machine wheels by one setting (from #0 to #1, in this case) and repeat to roll out the sheet again. Repeat these steps until the pasta sheet has reached your desired thinness. If following the thickness setting in one of the following recipes, be sure to check the settings of your machine for the equivalent setting.

At a certain point, the pasta usually becomes too long to comfortably handle and manage. Feel free to cut the sheet in half when necessary and continue to roll out each piece separately.

If you're making ribbon pasta, such as tagliatelle, set up the cutter attachment as directed by the manufacturer of your machine. Dust it with flour before inserting the edge of a pasta sheet while cranking inward. Dust the cut pasta with flour before arranging it on a baking sheet or platter while you finish the rest of the dough.

HOW TO COOK PASTA

Cooking pasta is one of those basic kitchen skills that seems obvious and impossible to mess up yet is the source of the most egregious mistakes holding back home cooks from phenomenal Italian food. Here, we go back to the basics to explain the ins and outs of this misunderstood process.

The Water

No one likes pasta that sticks and clumps together. To remedy this common problem, many recipes call for the addition of olive oil into the pasta water. This is, pure and simple, a waste of precious oil. Olive oil will only float to the top of the water and do nothing to prevent sticking.

The real culprit behind sticky pasta is not using enough water. Pasta should have plenty of room to dance; it should never overcrowd the pot. Measuring pasta water is a bit silly, so we don't recommend doing so. Instead, just be sure to use plenty of water and err on the side of cooking in a pot that's a little too big rather than too small.

Bring the water to a nice, rolling boil before adding . . .

The Salt

Pasta, like every ingredient, needs salt to bring out its natural flavor. Too many people think of pasta as a bland, tasteless canvas. It needs seasoning to taste good, and a tiny pinch of salt in the water does absolutely nothing. Pasta absorbs salt as it boils, so remember that most of the sodium you add will remain in the water and generous amounts are needed.

Like pasta water, we think that measuring salt is a needless exercise; instead, salting should be done by taste. Start by generously salting the water before or after it comes to a boil with a small palmful of coarse sea salt. (Contrary to popular belief, it makes no noticeable difference whether the water is salted before or after it comes to a boil.) Larger quantities cooked in bigger stockpots will obviously require one or two palmfuls more. Don't worry; we'll return to the subject shortly and explain how to adjust and re-salt the pasta later to taste.

Adding the Pasta

Now we come to the part that varies depending on the type of pasta you're cooking. Short pasta (such as penne or rigatoni) can simply be dumped straight into the water. With long, dry pasta (like spaghetti), you may encounter a scenario in which the pasta is too long to fit sideways into the pot. Whatever you do, don't break the pasta! Spaghetti is long for a reason; if it was meant to be shorter, it would have come in the box that way.

To add long pasta into a narrower pot, hold the pasta in a bundle and place it straight down into one of the bottom corners of the pot. The top edges of the pasta will lean against the opposing rim. Let it sit for about 20 to 30 seconds. After this time, the pasta will soften enough that you can gently push it down into the water using a wooden spoon or other utensil.

Adding fresh pasta into a pot is quite simple. In the case of ribbons, such as tagliatelle, simply scoop them up in big handfuls and drop them in. Delicate pasta shapes, such as gnocchi, sometimes require being lifted up on a towel and carefully poured into the water, but we've noted these instances in the recipes. Don't worry about excess flour from fresh pasta being added to the water; it will just make your pasta creamier in the end. As soon as you add any pasta into a pot of water, gently stir it to prevent sticking.

Boiling the Pasta

Just keep an eye on the pasta and stir it occasionally as it cooks.

The Timing

Pasta should be served "al dente," meaning it's fully cooked through but still retains a satisfying bite. It shouldn't be soft and mushy. Store-bought pasta has an estimated cook time (e.g., 10 to 12 minutes) on the package, and we generally find that the lowest number is pretty spot-on. However, this doesn't mean you should just set a timer and forget about it.

It's important to learn how to judge pasta doneness by taste. This skill is a must if you make your own pasta, as there isn't a box with instructions to reference. Also, a lot of pasta recipes call for finishing the pasta in a pan or pot with the sauce, meaning that the pasta needs to be drained a few minutes before it reaches al dente doneness. The recipes in this book point out these instances but be prepared to boil pasta for several minutes less than what the package says. A timer will be little help when finishing pasta in a pan with sauce, so you'll need to develop the skill of cooking to taste.

Fresh pasta boils much faster than dry pasta. In the case of ribbon pasta, such as tagliatelle, a cook time of 2 to 3 minutes is usually all that is needed for al dente noodles. Thicker pasta will need a little more time, and very thin fresh pasta can cook in as little as 30 seconds. Homemade pasta doesn't come with manufacturer-tested instructions, which is why it's even more important to learn about . . .

Tasting the Pasta

As the pasta nears completion (usually about 2 minutes before you expect it to be ready with dry pasta and about 30 seconds before if making fresh pasta), it's time to start tasting it. Use tongs or a slotted spoon to pull out a single piece and (carefully, because it's hot) eat it. Tasting the pasta is important for two reasons.

First, it's the only way to really know how cooked it is. Check the texture and bite. Is it still raw inside? Is the bite pleasant? With a little practice, you'll quickly develop the ability to taste a piece of pasta and be able to estimate how much longer it needs to cook before it's al dente. Remember that pasta doneness is a subjective matter, so all you need to know is what *you* like.

The second reason is to taste for salt. The pasta should taste seasoned; it should have flavor. It should taste good enough that you could drain it, mix it with some olive oil, and enjoy a great plate of pasta. If you find it lacking, add more salt to the water as the pasta finishes cooking.

Draining the Pasta

There are very few instances when pasta should be fully drained in a colander, the most common method. Doing so unnecessarily dirties an extra dish and wastes the precious, starchy pasta water, an invaluable ingredient when mixing pasta with sauce. There are a few exceptions, such as when the pasta is heading into a more liquid sauce (such as Ragù alla Napoletana on page 81). If you do drain the pasta completely, be sure to scoop up and set aside a cup of the pasta water in advance so that you have some handy should you need it.

Usually, the best way to "drain" pasta is to scoop it up with a utensil and transfer it directly into the saucepan or pot. The best tool for the job will vary, depending on the pasta shape. Use tongs or a spaghetti fork for long pasta and a slotted spoon for short pasta.

Putting It All Together

Perhaps the single biggest pasta mistake is serving boiled pasta with a big ladleful of sauce on top. Pasta needs to be thoroughly mixed—usually cooked— with the sauce into a unified dish. In most cases, this means transferring slightly undercooked pasta into a pan of sauce and cooking both together while stirring vigorously, until the pasta is evenly coated in sauce and al dente.

If the pasta needs more time to reach complete doneness, you can easily extend its cook time by spooning some pasta water into the pan and continuing cooking it. In this way, the pasta is finished like a risotto, and you can precisely cook it to a doneness you prefer. Just be sure to allow the excess liquid to thicken at the end so that the sauce isn't too soupy.

Serving

This part is simple, but important: pasta should be served and eaten immediately. Nothing is worse than cold pasta, so don't let it sit around. In fact, there is an accepted rule in Italy that dining guests should dig into their pasta right away, even if others are still waiting for their plates to come out of the kitchen.

HOW TO MAKE POTATO GNOCCHI

Potato gnocchi are pasta dumplings made with flour and mashed potatoes. They're extremely versatile and, when properly made, have a light, fluffy texture that's to die for. Gnocchi are one of the most commonly and consistently butchered pasta types, due to the misconception that the dough requires egg. While the addition of an egg or two does indeed make the pasta easier to make, the dough will become too dense and chewy. Take the time to learn the real method, and you will be rewarded with an extraordinary pasta.

Unlike normal fresh pasta, gnocchi dough should be worked and kneaded as little as possible. Don't be afraid to work in the flour, but you shouldn't knead it much beyond the point when you achieve a good texture. Flour must be added by feeling, as no two potatoes have the same moisture levels. Try to add just enough flour so that the dough isn't sticky, but no more. The less flour you add, the fluffier your gnocchi will be.

Regarding the potatoes, try to use some that have been sitting around for a few days and have therefore lost some moisture. As the saying goes, "Old potatoes make good gnocchi." If the potatoes are too wet and fresh, you risk the gnocchi dissolving while boiling. If all you have are very fresh potatoes, you can remedy the problem by incorporating a little bit of extra flour into the dough. The pasta will be denser, but at least it will remain intact.

Gnocchi are best served with simple sauces that let the potato flavor shine through, such as our Simple Tomato Sauce (page 32). Because the dumplings are delicate, it's best to gently mix them with the sauce in a large bowl with a rubber spatula, rather than in a hot pan. For a phenomenal baked gnocchi dish, try Gnocchi alla Sorrentina (page 111).

DURATION: About 2 hours, depending on the quantity you make and the shaping method you choose

Russet potatoes (about 7 ounces, or 200 g, per desired serving), skins on

All-purpose flour, as needed (there is no suggested amount, but have plenty on hand)

Salt

1. Place the potatoes in a large pot of water. Bring the water to a boil and let the potatoes cook until they are fork-tender, 45 to 60 minutes. Drain and let cool until the potatoes are still hot, but you can comfortably handle them. Peel the potatoes with a paring knife; the skins should easily pull off.

2. Using a potato masher, ricer, or vegetable mill, mash the potatoes, then place them directly onto a large, clean work surface. Dust the potatoes generously with a large handful of flour and begin kneading them together into a dough. As you knead, continue to dust the potatoes with more flour until the dough is no longer sticky. At this point, stop kneading or adding flour. (Be careful, because it's possible to keep kneading the potatoes until they become sticky again, creating an endless loop of flour addition. Try to stop adding flour as soon as the dough doesn't stick, and the mixture seems like it can be molded and shaped.)

3. As you make the gnocchi, dust the dough, work surface, tools, and formed gnocchi often and liberally with more flour. (It is very important to prevent sticking, and dusting will keep everything dry without incorporating more flour directly into the dough.) It is easiest to work in batches, so cut a manageable chunk of dough off from the rest and roll it under your palms into a long snake, about the width of a ring finger. Make sure the diameter of the strand is even and consistent. Using a bench scraper or knife, cut the strand into small pieces about 1 inch (2.5 cm) in length.

4. You can either cook the gnocchi as is or use a fingertip to press a hole in the center of each piece to help hold sauce. For extra-fancy gnocchi, use a fingertip or the side of your thumb to press and roll each piece across the surface of a gnocchi board—a small, handheld wooden board with a ridged surface. This will result in a hole on one side and ridges on the other.

5. Arrange the finished gnocchi on a clean towel dusted liberally with flour. Keep each gnocco separated so that they do not touch and stick. Repeat the shaping steps until all the dough has been formed into gnocchi.

6. To cook fresh gnocchi, bring a large pot of water to a boil and salt it generously. Gather the edges of the towel together to lift the gnocchi and pour them into the water. Stir them very gently to prevent sticking. After cooking for just 1 or 2 minutes, the gnocchi will float and rise to the surface of the water. Skim them off with a slotted spoon and transfer to the sauce of your choice.

HOW TO MAKE A SIMPLE TOMATO SAUCE

A simple tomato sauce is one of the most basic building blocks of Italian cuisine. It is an incredible pasta sauce, a base for many baked dishes, and even a medium for cooking meatballs (see Polpette al Sugo on page 149) and other meat. However, it's also one of the easiest dishes to mess up through over-complication.

Try to avoid the temptation to add a bunch of extra seasoning to this. Carrots, onion, spices, and so on will just end up destroying the refreshing flavor this sauce provides. If you salt it well, you'll be amazed at how much flavor can be produced by just tomatoes, olive oil, basil, and the smallest hint of garlic.

DURATION: 30 to 40 minutes ◆ YIELD: About 3 cups (720 ml)

28 ounces (800 g) canned whole peeled tomatoes

1 clove garlic, peeled

¼ cup (60 ml) extra-virgin olive oil

4 or 5 fresh basil leaves

Salt

1. Add the tomatoes, garlic, olive oil, and basil to a large pot or saucepan over medium heat. Bring to a gentle simmer and lightly season the sauce with salt (but be careful here; the sauce will concentrate, and you can always add more later).

2. After a few minutes of cooking, the whole tomatoes will have softened enough that you can break them up into a pulp with a fork. Do so and let the sauce simmer, partially covered, for 25 to 30 minutes, until it thickens to your taste. If necessary, add some water to thin out the sauce and cook it longer.

3. Remove and discard the garlic clove, then season with salt again before turning off the heat.

4. Use the sauce immediately, or let it cool to room temperature, then store it in an airtight container in the refrigerator for about 1 week or freeze for up to 3 months.

HOW TO MAKE BESCIAMELLA

This simple sauce is a basic building block of many baked pasta dishes, most notably Lasagna alla Bolognese (page 120). In that case it's paired with a ragù, but besciamella is perhaps most often used for white baked pasta when a substitute is needed for tomato. With a tangy taste but a relatively low fat content, it adds creamy texture without dulling the flavor of other ingredients.

DURATION: 45 ♦ YIELD: 4 cups (1 L)

7 tablespoons (100 g) unsalted butter
¾ cup plus 1½ tablespoons (100 g) all-purpose flour
4¼ cups (1 L) whole milk, at room temperature (see Note)
Pinch of ground nutmeg
Salt and freshly ground black pepper

1. In a large saucepan, melt the butter over low heat, then immediately whisk in the flour. Stir constantly; a thick roux will quickly form. Gradually add the milk while continuing to whisk.

2. When all the milk has been added and the flour is completely dissolved, add the nutmeg and a pinch each of salt and pepper. Increase the heat to medium-low and continue to stir until the milk thickens into a gravy-like consistency. (Be patient; it can take about 30 minutes to reduce depending on the starting temperature of the milk). As the besciamella nears completion, season it again with salt and pepper.

3. Use the sauce immediately, or let it cool to room temperature and keep it covered until ready to use.

4. Store in an airtight container in the refrigerator for up to 2 days. It is perfectly normal for a skin to develop on the surface of the sauce; just pick it out and discard before using.

NOTE *While you can make besciamella with cold milk, using room-temperature milk will greatly speed up the thickening process, so consider taking it out of the refrigerator 30 minutes prior to cooking.*

HOW TO FRY AT HOME

Deep-frying is a fundamental cooking skill that is rarely practiced at home in much of the modern world, largely due to an unwarranted demonization and a tendency to overcomplicate the process. Contrary to popular belief, properly fried food does not absorb an excessive amount of oil and fat. No one bats an eye at a bruschetta drizzled in olive oil, which, bite for bite, is certain to contain more added fat than a deep-fried cutlet.

Frying is simple and requires no special equipment. All you need is frying oil, a suitably sized pot or pan, and (perhaps) a slotted spoon.

In general, vegetable oils are perfectly fine for use in most deep-frying. In Italy, sunflower and peanut oils are most commonly used. Canola also works, although we're of the opinion that it doesn't smell great, so we avoid it. In some rare cases in which the oil is intentionally allowed to soak into the food (such as Pasta alla Norma on page 108), extra-virgin olive oil is a must and noted in the recipes. Here are the steps for frying at home:

1. Use a wide, deep pan for frying flat foods that require a lot of horizontal space (such as vegetable slices), and a deeper, narrower pot for chunkier foods that need to be submerged (such as Arancini on page 50). Fill the pan or pot with just enough oil to submerge the food you are frying and be sure to account for displacement when you add the food into the oil (i.e., don't overfill the pot).

2. Give the oil plenty of time to come up to temperature over medium-high heat. While many recipes call for a very strict and specific oil temperature that must be maintained, the truth is that a thermometer is no more necessary for deep-frying than for sautéing. We never use one, nor have we ever seen a traditional Italian cook use one.

3. To see if the oil is hot enough to fry, simply drop a small morsel of the food you're frying into the pot. Bread crumbs are great for this and often handy when frying, but just about anything will work. Use a tiny pinch of meat if making polpette for Polpette al Sugo (page 149), a little piece of eggplant for Parmigiana di Melanzane (page 144), a grain of cooked rice for Crocchette di Riso (page 42), and so on.

If, immediately upon contact with the oil, the morsel starts to bubble furiously, the oil is ready. If it takes a second or two to start bubbling or sinks to the bottom and does nothing, the oil needs more time or more heat.

4. When the oil is ready, carefully drop the food in or gently lower it into the pot with a slotted spoon. It's important not to overcrowd the pan, which is why we almost always recommend frying in batches. Doing so will also limit the amount of oil and the size of pot needed.

If, while frying, you find that the oil starts to bubble and splash out of the pot, that's simply a sign that you need to turn down the heat a little bit; conversely, if the food bubbles a little sluggishly and is taking a while to cook, turn up the heat slightly.

It's important to turn and flip the food while frying so that it cooks evenly, especially in the case of ingredients that float on the surface, such as vegetable slices. Do so with a couple of forks. When the food is golden brown on all sides, remove it from the oil with a slotted spoon and transfer to a paper towel–lined plate to drain.

5. Most fried food should be salted after frying, not before. Sprinkle it lightly with salt and enjoy.

6. Many people save frying oil and reuse it later. We don't, but you certainly can. If you choose to do so, let the oil cool completely, then filter it into a sealable container. To dispose of frying oil, let it cool to room temperature, then pour it back into the bottle it came in (or another sealable container) with a funnel and place it in the trash.

As with all heat-related food prep, be cautious at all times.

Dasà, Calabria: Eva's hometown.

FRITTI

⇥ **Fried Appetizers & Street Food** ⇤

*Most Italian antipasti, or appetizers, are simply
ingredients and products that are snacked on
by themselves, such as sliced prosciutto and
cheeses. There is, however, a whole class of fried
finger-food treats that are usually served on
giant platters before a large feast or wrapped in
paper from street vendors.*

FRITTELLE DI ZUCCHINE

⤚ *Fried Zucchini Fritters* ⤙

One of our favorite fried treats is a fritter made with zucchini flowers battered in flour and carbonated water. Eva's mother, Mamma Rosa, is a master of this delicacy, and we get quite excited when we see a crate of zucchini blossoms appear in her pantry. Part of our excitement is because we're rarely able to replicate the recipe in the United States, where zucchini flowers are hard to come by. Luckily, the same technique can be applied to thinly sliced zucchini fruit, a much more accessible option. While these fritters may lack the exotic flavor of the flowers, they are almost as delicious and very simple to make.

DURATION: 1 hour
YIELD: 10 to 12 fritters

9 ounces (255 g) zucchini, very thinly sliced

Salt

1 cup (120 g) all-purpose flour

2/3 cup (160 ml) chilled carbonated water

Pinch of freshly ground black pepper

Vegetable oil, for frying

1. Place the zucchini slices in a large bowl and sprinkle them with salt. Mix them by hand so that they are evenly salted, then let sit for 30 minutes to release excess water.

2. In a separate large bowl, thoroughly mix the flour, carbonated water, black pepper, and a pinch of salt.

3. Drain the zucchini slices and squeeze out as much moisture as possible. Mix the zucchini into the batter.

4. Fill a large, deep pan with 1 inch (2.5 cm) of vegetable oil and heat to frying temperature (see How to Fry at Home on page 34).

5. Using two spoons, carefully drop a heaping spoonful of battered zucchini into the hot oil. As soon as it is in the oil, use the two spoons to spread it into a flat disc (don't worry about the shape being perfect). You can add more fritters into the pan and fry several at the same time; just be careful not to overcrowd the pan. Fry the fritters, flipping occasionally, until golden on both sides. Remove with a slotted spoon to a paper towel–lined plate to drain.

6. Serve warm and fresh.

CROCCHETTE DI RISO

⇥ *Rice Croquettes* ⇤

These fried rice croquettes are a specialty of Eva's mother and a treat that friends and neighbors gleefully look forward to eating at every family gathering, holiday, or any other event where she has an excuse to cook them. Mamma Rosa's secret is simple: plenty of cheese. How much? Hard to say (she won't), but the more you add, the closer you'll likely come to her delicious result.

DURATION: 1 hour

YIELD: About 10 crocchette

Salt

⅔ cup (150 g) arborio, vialone nano, or carnaroli rice

2½ ounces (70 g) Parmigiano-Reggiano cheese, or to taste, grated

2½ ounces (70 g) pecorino cheese, or to taste, grated

1 or 2 large eggs

1 tablespoon (3.5 g) chopped parsley

Freshly ground black pepper

Fine bread crumbs

Extra-virgin olive or vegetable oil, for frying

1. Bring a medium pot of water to a boil, and salt it generously. Add the rice and cook as directed on the package until al dente to your taste. Drain the rice and transfer it to a large bowl. While it is hot, thoroughly stir in the grated cheeses, 1 egg, the parsley, plenty of black pepper, and a pinch of salt. Add another egg if the mix feels too dry and crumbly; conversely, if it feels too wet and sticky, add more cheese. Let the mixture cool for 1 or 2 minutes before proceeding to form the crocchette.

2. Fill a large plate with bread crumbs. Wet your hands and scoop up about ¼ cup (60 g) of the rice mixture and roll it by hand into a small torpedo shape about 3 inches (7.5 cm) in length. Make sure that it is smooth, with no visible cracks or gaps. Dust the crocchetta in the bread crumbs until it is completely and evenly coated. Set aside on a plate and repeat until you have used all the rice.

3. Fill a large, deep pan with about 2 inches (5 cm) of oil and bring it up to frying temperature (see How to Fry at Home on page 34).

4. Working in batches so as not to overcrowd the pan, carefully drop the crocchette in the hot oil and fry until golden brown, turning them with two forks so that they fry evenly on all sides. Carefully remove them with a slotted spoon to a paper towel–lined plate to drain.

5. Serve warm and fresh.

CROCCHETTE DI PATATE

⊰ *Potato Croquettes* ⊱

Crispy on the outside, soft and cheesy on the inside, these fried potato crocchette are irresistible. While these are savory, here's an interesting trick we learned from Mamma Rosa to turn them into a dessert: cut a lengthwise incision in a crocchetta, open it like a hot-dog bun, and sprinkle in some sugar. It sounds weird, but it's delicious! Like with making gnocchi (page 30), it's best to use potatoes that have been lying around in your pantry for a few days, as they will be drier. Fresh, wet potatoes risk breaking apart when frying. We recommend using a vegetable mill for making mashed potatoes, but feel free to use a ricer or hand masher if that's all you have.

DURATION: 1½ hours, largely unattended

YIELD: About 15 crocchette

2 large russet potatoes, skins on

7 ounces (200 g) Parmigiano-Reggiano cheese, or to taste, grated

Salt and freshly ground black pepper

1 or 2 large eggs

All-purpose flour

Extra-virgin olive or vegetable oil, for frying

1. Place the potatoes in a large pot of water. Bring the water to a boil and let the potatoes cook until fork-tender, 45 to 60 minutes, depending on the size of the potatoes. Drain the potatoes, let them cool to the touch, and peel them with a paring knife. Place the potatoes in a large bowl and mash using your preferred method.

2. Add the grated cheese and season with salt and pepper. Thoroughly mix in 1 egg; the mixture should be soft and tacky enough to mold without being wet and sticky. If the potatoes are too dry and crumbly, mix in another egg to hold it together.

3. Fill a large plate with flour. Scoop up about ¼ cup (60 g) of potato mixture and roll it into a torpedo shape about 3 inches (7.5 cm) in length. Make sure it is very smooth. Dust the crocchette in the flour until it is completely and evenly coated. Set aside on a plate and repeat until you have used all the potato mixture.

4. Fill a large, deep pan with about 3 inches (7.5 cm) of oil and bring it up to frying temperature (see How to Fry at Home on page 34).

5. Working in batches so as not to overcrowd the pan, carefully drop the crocchette in the hot oil and fry until golden and crispy on all sides, turning them often with a fork. Remove with a slotted spoon to a paper towel–lined plate to drain.

6. Serve warm and fresh.

SUPPLÌ

⤐| *Roman Stuffed Rice Croquettes* |⤐

Supplì are Rome's answer to Sicilian Arancini (page 50). Unlike the latter, supplì are made by cooking the rice directly in the ragù. You will definitely find yourself tempted to just eat the "ragù risotto" as it is, but hold firm and continue on to the frying stage. You'll thank us once you bite into a crispy crocchetta stuffed with gooey mozzarella cheese.

DURATION: 4 hours, largely unattended

YIELD: 18 to 20 supplì

---

3 tablespoons (45 ml) extra-virgin olive oil, plus more for frying

¼ large white onion, diced

1 pound (450 g) ground beef

Pinch of freshly ground black pepper

Salt

½ cup (120 ml) white wine

2 cups (480 ml) tomato puree

1½ cups (350 g) carnaroli or arborio rice

3½ ounces (100 g) pecorino cheese, grated

2 tablespoons (30 g) unsalted butter

5 large eggs

Bread crumbs

8 ounces (225 g) mozzarella cheese, chopped

1. In a medium saucepan, combine the 3 tablespoons olive oil and onion over medium heat and cook, stirring frequently for 3 to 4 minutes, until the onion is tender. Add the ground beef and cook until browned, breaking it up into a fine crumble with a wooden spoon as it cooks. Stir in the pepper and season with salt.

2. Add the wine and bring the ragù to a simmer. Cook until the smell of alcohol has dissipated, 4 to 5 minutes. Add the tomato puree and season with a generous sprinkle of salt. Bring the ragù to a simmer again and cook, partially covered, for 45 minutes.

3. Stir the rice directly into the ragù and cook, stirring frequently, until al dente to your taste. (Most Italian rice varieties cook in 15 to 20 minutes; consult the instructions on the package.) The rice needs liquid to cook in, so add warm water as necessary to maintain a gentle simmer. When the rice is nearing completion, stop adding water so that the ragù can thicken.

4. When the rice is cooked, turn off the heat and stir in the pecorino and butter. Spread the rice mixture evenly in a large, rimmed baking sheet and let cool completely—about 2 hours at room temperature—before proceeding to form the supplì.

5. Crack the eggs into a small bowl and whisk until beaten. Fill a separate small bowl with bread crumbs.

6. Wet your hands and scoop up a large handful of rice and flatten it into your palm. Press a shallow depression into the center and place a generous pinch of chopped mozzarella inside. Cover with another handful of rice and press the supplì closed into a smooth, elongated torpedo.

continued on following page >>

7. Roll the torpedo first in the beaten eggs, then in the bread crumbs, taking care to coat it well with both. For extra crispiness, repeat these steps a second time. Place the finished supplì on a clean surface or baking sheet and repeat until you have used all the rice.

8. Fill a large, deep pan with about 3 inches (7.5 cm) of olive oil and bring it up to frying temperature (see How to Fry at Home on page 34). Working in batches of 2 or 3 suppli at a time, carefully drop them into the hot oil and fry until golden on all sides, turning frequently with two forks to cook them evenly. Remove with a slotted spoon to a paper towel-lined plate to drain. Let cool for a few minutes.

9. Serve warm and fresh.

BACCALÀ FRITTO IN PASTELLA

⇥ *Fried Salted Cod* ⇤

Baccalà is salted cod, a popular and often expensive delicacy in Italy. Ironically, this treat was originally a very economical way for poor Italians to preserve fish in days when fresh seafood was harder to come by. Because the Catholic Church discouraged the eating of meat on Christmas Eve, baccalà became one of the most popular holiday dishes. Even today, Italians grumble about having to reserve their salted cod weeks in advance, or else risk a baccalà-free Christmas. While this ingredient isn't always readily available, you can find it in many Italian markets. Some online sources ship it, as well. Fried baccalà is somewhere between an antipasto and a second course. Feel free to serve it as a snack or by itself as a complete dish.

DURATION: 20 minutes, plus some prep 3 days in advance

YIELD: 4 to 6 servings

1¾ pounds (800 g) baccalà

1¼ cups (150 g) plus 2 tablespoons (15 g) all-purpose flour, divided

⅔ cup (150 ml) chilled carbonated water

Pinch of salt

Vegetable oil, for frying

1. In order to avoid eating a veritable salt bomb, baccalà needs to be carefully prepared prior to cooking. Three days in advance, run the fish under cold tap water for 10 minutes. Let the baccalà soak in cold water (no need to keep it in the refrigerator) for the next 3 days, replacing the water once a day. After soaking, cut the baccalà into roughly 3-inch (7.5 cm) cubes.

2. In a medium bowl, whisk 1¼ cups (150 g) of the flour with the chilled carbonated water. Stir in the salt and place the batter in the freezer for 10 minutes.

3. While the batter chills, fill a large, deep pan with about 4 inches (10 cm) of vegetable oil. (The pan doesn't have to be wide, just deep, so feel free to use a narrow pot to minimize the amount of oil needed.) Heat the oil to frying temperature (see How to Fry at Home on page 34).

4. Meanwhile, toss the baccalà pieces in the remaining 2 tablespoons (15 g) flour so that they are lightly coated on all sides.

5. Dip a piece of fish in the chilled batter, then immediately (and carefully) drop it into the hot oil. Fry for 6 to 8 minutes, until the outside is golden and crispy. Remove with a slotted spoon to a paper towel-lined plate to drain. Fry the baccalà in batches so as not to overcrowd the pan.

6. Sprinkle the fried baccalà with salt and serve hot and fresh.

MONTANARINA

⤜ *Miniature Fried Pizza* ⤛

One of the most famous Neapolitan street foods is pizza fritta, or fried pizza. Ironically, this classic dish doesn't resemble a pizza at all; it looks more like a huge fried calzone. While pizza fritta can be made at home, it's a bit daunting, as it requires a fairly large frying station with lots of oil. An easier option, that's just as delicious, is to make montanara, or the miniature montanarina, in this case, which looks like a pizza but with fried dough as the base. The dough is a normal pizza dough, and the toppings can theoretically be the same as any pizza toppings. With this margherita version, we recommend substituting the mozzarella with Parmigiano, as it will not require re-cooking to melt.

DURATION: 1 hour, plus 15 hours rising for the dough

YIELD: 6 montanarina

¾ teaspoon (3 g) active dry yeast

½ cup plus 2 tablespoons (150 ml) room-temperature water

2 cups (250 g) Manitoba or bread flour, plus more for dusting

2 teaspoons (10 g) salt

Vegetable or other neutral oil, for frying

¾ cup (180 ml) Simple Tomato Sauce (page 32)

Grated Parmigiano-Reggiano cheese

6 fresh basil leaves

1. In a large bowl, combine the yeast with the water and stir until the yeast dissolves completely. Gradually add the flour while mixing by hand. When all the flour is added and a rough dough begins to form, mix in the salt.

2. Transfer the dough to a lightly floured surface and gently fold it in half about 10 times. Dust the inside of the same bowl with flour, place the dough ball back in, and cover the bowl with plastic wrap or a lid. Refrigerate for 12 hours. Remove the dough bowl from the refrigerator and let the dough rise at room temperature for 2 hours.

3. On a floured surface, cut the dough into 6 equal portions and form each one into a smooth ball. Hold a ball in your hands and gently pull and tuck any rough edges underneath so that the top becomes smooth and even. Repeat with the remaining dough balls. Place them on a floured baking sheet, leaving about 3 inches (7.5 cm) between them. Cover with plastic wrap and let the dough rise at room temperature for 1 hour.

4. Fill a small pot with about 2 inches (5 cm) of oil and bring up to frying temperature (see How to Fry at Home on page 34). Remove a ball from the baking sheet and gently flatten it into a disc with your fingers. Carefully drop it into the hot oil; the dough will quickly puff up like a balloon as it cooks. Turn the dough over frequently and carefully baste it with oil using a spoon. When golden brown, remove it with a slotted spoon to a paper towel–lined plate to drain. Repeat with the remaining dough balls. Gently press down the puffed-up centers of the fried dough balls. Fill the depressions with a few spoonfuls of tomato sauce and top with a generous grating of Parmigiano and a single basil leaf.

5. Serve warm and fresh.

ARANCINI

⤜ *Sicilian Stuffed Rice Balls* ⤛

One can't think of southern Italian street food without these Sicilian fried rice balls coming to mind. There are a few different types of arancini (or *arancine* as they're called in western Sicily), but the most classic is filled with a thick, meaty ragù. It's a treat that must be sought out hot and fresh, which is why many tourists are disappointed after selecting an arancino that has been sitting on a rosticceria shelf for several hours. One must either learn from the locals where to buy fresh ones or make them yourself.

DURATION: 4 hours, largely unattended

YIELD: 12 to 15 arancini

3 tablespoons (45 ml) extra-virgin olive oil

¼ large white onion, diced

½ large carrot, diced

½ rib celery, diced

4 ounces (115 g) ground beef

4 ounces (115 g) ground pork

2 bay leaves

Pinch of ground cloves

5 teaspoons (25 g) salt, plus more to taste

Freshly ground black pepper

¼ cup (60 ml) white wine

2 tablespoons (30 g) tomato paste

1 cup (240 ml) warm water

⅓ cup (45 g) frozen peas

½ cup (50 g) grated caciocavallo or sharp provolone cheese

2 cups (500 g) arborio rice (see Note opposite)

¼ teaspoon (0.25 g) saffron

¼ cup (60 g) unsalted butter

⅔ cup (85 g) all-purpose flour

Bread crumbs

Vegetable oil, for frying

1. In a medium saucepan, heat the olive oil over medium heat. Add the onion, carrot, and celery and cook, stirring frequently, for 3 to 4 minutes, until the onion is tender. Add the ground meat and cook until browned, breaking it up into a fine crumble with a wooden spoon as it cooks. Stir in the bay leaves and cloves and season to taste with salt and pepper.

2. Add the wine and bring the ragù to a simmer. Let simmer for 4 to 5 minutes, until most of the excess liquid has evaporated. Meanwhile, in a small bowl or measuring cup, dissolve the tomato paste in the warm water. Once the wine has cooked off, stir the diluted tomato paste into the ragù.

3. Partially cover the pot and bring the sauce to a gentle simmer over medium-low heat. Let simmer, stirring occasionally, for 30 minutes. Stir in the frozen peas and let simmer for an additional 30 minutes, or until the liquid has thickened; the ragù should be quite dry. Turn off the heat and stir in the cheese. Let the sauce cool to room temperature.

4. While the ragù cooks, combine the rice, saffron, butter, and 5 teaspoons (25 g) salt with 4 cups (960 ml) of water in a medium pot. Bring the water to a simmer, stirring frequently. Cover the pot and let cook until the rice has fully absorbed all the liquid, 15 to 20 minutes. Spread the rice flat in a large, rimmed baking sheet and let cool to room temperature.

5. Place the flour in a bowl and mix in just enough water to make a thin batter. Fill a large plate with bread crumbs.

6. Begin by wetting your hands to prevent sticking. Scoop up a large handful of rice, then flatten it into your palm. Press a shallow depression into the center and place a heaping tablespoon of ragù inside. Cover the ragù with another handful of rice and press the arancino closed into a smooth, round ball. Roll the ball first in the batter, then in the bread crumbs, taking care to coat the ball well with both. Place the arancino on a clean surface or baking sheet and repeat until you have used up all the rice and/or ragù.

7. Fill a large, deep pan with 4 inches (10 cm) of vegetable oil and heat it to frying temperature (see How to Fry at Home on page 34). Working in batches of 2 or 3 arancini at a time, carefully drop them into the hot oil and fry until golden on all sides, turning frequently with two forks to cook them evenly. Remove with a slotted spoon to a paper towel–lined plate to drain. Let cool for a few minutes.

8. Serve warm and fresh.

NOTE *Usually, the most common Italian rice varieties (arborio, carnaroli, vialone nano, etc.) are interchangeable. In this case, stick to arborio. It's a bit starchier, which will help to hold the arancini balls together.*

CALAMARI FRITTI

⇥ *Fried Squid* ⇤

Fried calamari is a beloved appetizer around the world, but Italians are often left scratching their heads at the thick batters and heavy dipping sauces that too often mask the beautiful simplicity of this dish. The secret to incredible calamari fritti is a light flour breading and the simplest seafood condiment of all: lemon juice.

DURATION: 30 minutes

YIELD: 4 servings

About 2 cups (240 g) all-purpose flour

Extra-virgin olive or vegetable oil (we recommend EVOO), for frying

1 pound (450 g) squid, cleaned and prepped (see Note)

Salt

Lemon wedges, for serving

1. Place the flour on a large plate or in a shallow bowl.

2. Fill a large, deep pan with 3 inches (7.5 cm) of oil and bring up to frying temperature (see How to Fry at Home on page 34).

3. Working in batches so as not to overcrowd the pan, take a large handful of squid pieces and thoroughly dredge them in the flour so that each piece is completely coated. Carefully drop them into the hot oil one piece at a time to avoid them sticking together.

4. Gently turn and stir the squid until they have a golden, crispy exterior. Use a slotted spoon to remove to a paper towel–lined plate to drain. Repeat with the remaining squid.

5. Sprinkle the calamari generously with salt and serve with lemon wedges.

NOTE *Often, squid is sold already prepared for frying, with the body cut into rings. If not, you can easily prep it yourself. Cut off the tentacles and leave them whole, then slice the body into 1-inch-thick (2.5 cm) rings.*

BREAD & PIZZA

No meal can be considered complete without bread. Not only is it a filling carb, but it also serves a very functional purpose at the table: mopping up the leftover sauce on a plate (this practice is called "scarpetta"). We have therefore devoted this chapter to the cornerstone of Italian food, along with its ever-popular cousin: pizza.

BASIC BREAD

Bread is the fundamental base of the Italian diet. Every meal is served with it. Perhaps the most important function of bread is to make the scarpetta. There are many kinds of bread in Italy; this is a very basic and easy recipe that will serve for most general purposes—from bruschetta to scarpetta.

DURATION: 3 to 4 hours, largely unattended

YIELD: 1 large loaf

=================

4⅛ cups (500 g) bread flour

1 teaspoon (4 g) active dry yeast

1⅔ cups (400 ml) room-temperature water

2 teaspoons (10 g) salt

Semolina flour, for dusting

1. In a large bowl, mix the flour and yeast. Gradually add the water while mixing with a wooden spoon. When most of the water is incorporated and a rough dough begins to form, mix in the salt. Add the remaining water and keep mixing until a sticky, even dough forms. Cover the bowl with plastic wrap and let rise for 30 minutes at room temperature.

2. Wet your hands to prevent the dough from sticking. Keeping it in the bowl, grab one edge of the dough, pull it up, and fold it over on top of itself. Repeat this several times, working your way around the dough to fold it several times in different directions. Finish by lifting the dough ball from the middle and letting it sag to fold itself in half. Set it back down in the bowl. Cover the bowl and let rise for 1 hour. Wet your hands again and repeat the previous folding steps. Cover the bowl and let the dough rise an additional 45 minutes.

3. Generously dust a large work surface with semolina flour. Flip the bowl upside down over the flour and let the dough fall out. As you work with the dough for the rest of the shaping process, handle it very gently and try not to squeeze or press it, as this will collapse the air pockets inside. Gently pull and stretch the edges of the dough so that it roughly forms a large rectangle, about 14 × 7 inches (35 × 18 cm). Fold it into thirds lengthwise, with one-third folded past the middle and the other folded on top; the dough should look like a big burrito. Take each end of the "burrito" and fold it inward so that the ends meet in the middle. Gently press them together. Cover the dough with a mixing bowl and let rest for 15 minutes. Meanwhile, preheat the oven to 480°F (250°C) and place a rack on the bottom.

4. Fold the dough in half lengthwise and gently pinch the edges sealed. Flip it upside down so that the smooth bottom is on top. Dust a baking sheet with semolina flour and place the dough on top, cover with the bowl again, and let rest for 10 minutes.

5. Using a clean, kitchen-only safety razor blade or sharp knife, slice a long, shallow incision along the top of the bread. Bake for 20 minutes on the bottom rack, then reduce the oven temperature to 410°F (210°C) and bake for an additional 30 minutes. Let cool for at least 1 hour before slicing and serving.

CIABATTA

⤛ *Panini Sandwich Bread* ⤜

Italian sandwiches are very simple, usually made with a couple of ingredients served in a bread roll. One of our favorites is so simple that anyone who hasn't tried it is sure to underestimate how delicious it is: thinly sliced mortadella and a drizzle of lemon juice. As always, simplicity requires good ingredients, and that certainly includes the bread. Ciabatta is a classic sandwich bread and perfect for making panini.

DURATION: 3½ hours, largely unattended

YIELD: 2 sandwich loaves

1½ teaspoons (5 g) active dry yeast

Pinch of granulated sugar

¾ cup plus 1½ tablespoons (200 ml) room-temperature water

1⅔ cups (250 g) all-purpose flour, plus more for dusting

Extra-virgin olive oil, for brushing

1½ teaspoons (8 g) salt

1. In a large bowl, stir the yeast and sugar with the water until both are dissolved. Add the flour and mix thoroughly with a wooden spoon; the dough should be very wet and sticky. Brush a separate large bowl with olive oil and transfer the dough to this bowl with a spatula. Cover the bowl with plastic wrap and let the dough rise at room temperature for 1½ hours.

2. After the dough has risen, add the salt and mix it in thoroughly with a wooden spoon.

3. Line a 9-inch (23 cm) square baking pan (or similar) with parchment paper so that the ends come up just over the edges of the pan, then brush the paper with a generous drizzle of oil. Pour the dough into the prepared pan and gently spread it out with a spatula until flat. Brush the top with more oil, loosely cover with plastic wrap, and let rise for 45 minutes.

4. Meanwhile, preheat the oven to 480°F (250°C). Place a small, oven-safe dish of water on the bottom rack to keep the oven moist.

5. Dust a large, clean work surface with plenty of flour. Transfer the dough to the center by lifting up the paper and carefully flipping it over onto the floured surface. Gently pull the dough out from the edges to form a large, flat square of dough, about 16 inches (40 cm). Sprinkle the top of the dough with more flour.

6. Using a bench scraper or knife, cut the dough in half; each half will become one ciabatta loaf. Grasp the nearest edge of one of the dough halves and fold it about one-quarter of the dough's length onto itself. Fold the doubled-up section forward 2 more times. While folding, use a bench scraper as necessary to detach any dough that might stick to the surface below. Repeat with the remaining dough half. Place the folded loaves on a nonstick baking sheet at least 3 inches (7.5 cm) apart.

7. Bake for 10 minutes, then reduce the temperature to 425°F (220°C) and bake for an additional 20 to 25 minutes, until the crust is deeply golden. Let cool completely before cutting and serving.

GRISSINI

⇥ *Breadsticks* ⇤

Breadsticks are definitely a traditional Italian recipe, but the real deal is a far cry from the doughy, buttery loaves that have come to be wrongly associated with Italian cuisine. Grissini were invented in Turin during the seventeenth century, apparently to settle the stomach of a young duke who couldn't digest soft bread. Naturally, these breadsticks aren't very bready at all; rather, they resemble long, crunchy crackers. The best grissini are immediately identifiable by their rustic, imperfect appearance: a sure sign of homemade quality.

DURATION: 3 hours

YIELD: About 40 breadsticks

---

2 cups (240 g) bread flour, plus more for dusting

1 teaspoon (4 g) active dry yeast

¾ cup (180 ml) room-temperature water

1½ teaspoons (8 g) salt

2 teaspoons extra-virgin olive oil, plus more for greasing and topping

6 teaspoons (18 g) sesame seeds, or to taste

Semolina flour, for dusting

1. Place the bread flour in a large bowl. In a small cup, stir the yeast with the water until it dissolves completely. Pour this into the flour and mix with a wooden spoon. When all the flour has dampened, add the salt and continue to mix. Once a rough dough forms, transfer it to a clean work surface. Flatten it with your hand, then drizzle the olive oil on top. Fold the oil in and begin kneading by hand.

2. Knead the dough for about 5 minutes. It will become quite sticky, and you may find it useful to "knead" with a bench scraper; to do so, slide the scraper underneath the dough, lift the edge up, and fold the dough on top of itself. Repeat from different angles, working your way around the dough to fold it in from all sides.

3. Once the oil is well incorporated, place a mixing bowl over the dough and let rest for 10 minutes.

4. After the dough has rested, scrape it off the counter and fold it several times by hand; do this by picking it up from the middle, folding it in half on itself as you set it back down, and then turning it 90 degrees and repeating. Fold the dough 6 to 8 times.

5. Place the dough into a mixing bowl, cover with plastic wrap, and let rise at room temperature for 1 to 1½ hours, until it has doubled in size.

continued on following page >>

6. Lightly dust a large work surface with bread flour and transfer the dough to the center. Use a rolling pin to roll out the dough into a large rectangle that can fit into a 9 × 13-inch (23 × 33 cm) baking pan (or similar). Lightly dust the dough with flour if it is too sticky to roll but try to use as little as possible.

7. Thoroughly brush the baking pan with olive oil, lay the dough rectangle inside, and spread it out by hand so that it fills every corner. Cover with plastic wrap and let rise at room temperature for 1 hour.

8. After it has risen, brush the entire surface of the dough with olive oil and sprinkle it evenly with sesame seeds. Use a bench scraper or knife to cut the dough into thin strips, widthwise, about ½ inch (13 mm) wide by 9 inches (23 cm) long. Now, cut all the strips in half with one lengthwise cut through the middle of the pan (perpendicular to the first cuts).

9. Preheat the oven to 355°F (180°C). Line two or three baking sheets with parchment paper (or bake in batches).

10. Spread a generous dusting of semolina flour on a work surface in front of you. Take piece of dough, hold it in the air, and gently twist the ends several times in opposing directions; the dough should naturally sag a bit and lengthen as it twists. Holding both ends of the breadstick, brush the dough through the semolina flour once before placing the breadstick on a prepared baking sheet. Repeat until all the dough is formed into breadsticks and arranged on baking sheets. (Keep them slightly separated to avoid sticking, but they won't rise.)

11. Bake for 15 to 20 minutes, until golden and crunchy.

12. Serve warm or at room temperature.

FOCACCIA GENOVESE

⤙ *Simple Focaccia Bread with Olive Oil & Salt* ⤚

Outside of Italy, this is perhaps the most famous and recognized version of focaccia. In its simplicity and flavor, it is a work of art, especially when made at home. Its crispy crust covered in pockets of salty olive oil makes it an irresistible treat. In Genoa, it is usually eaten for breakfast and dipped in coffee and milk.

DURATION: 4 to 5 hours, largely unattended

YIELD: 1 large focaccia

_____

1⅔ cups (200 g) all-purpose flour, plus more for dusting

1 cup (120 g) high-gluten flour (see Note opposite)

1¼ teaspoons (5 g) active dry yeast

¾ cup (180 ml) room-temperature water

3 teaspoons (15 g) salt, divided

1 teaspoon (7 g) honey

4 tablespoons extra-virgin olive oil, divided, plus more for brushing

1. In a large bowl, thoroughly mix the flours and yeast with a wooden spoon. Add the water, give it a quick mix, and then add 2 teaspoons (10 g) of the salt and the honey. Continue to mix until a very rough dough has formed.

2. Transfer the dough to a large, clean work surface and knead by hand until the dough is smooth and consistent. (It should not be sticky, but if it is, dust the dough with flour until it loses its tack.) Flatten the dough with your palm and pour 1 tablespoon (15 ml) of the olive oil on top. Fold in the oil and knead the dough until it is smooth and even. Form the dough into a ball and cover with a mixing bowl. Let rest for 30 minutes.

3. Flatten the dough into an oval-shaped pancake. Fold it widthwise in thirds (like folding paper for an envelope) so that it forms a small rectangle. Place it on a lightly floured surface, cover with a bowl again, and let rest for an additional 30 minutes.

4. Generously brush a large baking sheet with olive oil. Roll out the dough with a rolling pin until it is approximately ¾ inch (2 cm) thick, trying to keep it roughly in the shape of the baking sheet. Place the dough on the sheet, cover with plastic wrap, and let rest again for 30 minutes. After resting, the gluten in the dough should have relaxed enough that you can easily use your hands to spread it out more, filling the corners of the baking sheet. Be sure to press it firmly into the edges of the baking sheet so that the "crust" around the edge forms a slightly raised lip.

5. Lightly dust the top surface of the focaccia with flour and spread the flour evenly across it with your hand. Cover with plastic wrap and let rest for 1 hour.

6. Meanwhile, dissolve the remaining 1 teaspoon (5 g) salt in ⅓ cup (80 ml) of water.

7. After the dough has rested, it is time to make the characteristic dimples. Use your fingertips to press holes across the top of the focaccia. Drizzle the remaining 3 tablespoons (45 ml) olive oil on top, followed by a few spoonfuls of the salt water. Use your hands to evenly spread the olive oil and water across the focaccia. Add more salt water until each dimple has a small pool of liquid and oil inside. Let the focaccia rise, uncovered, for 45 minutes. Meanwhile, preheat the oven to 450°F (230°C).

8. Bake for 15 minutes, or until lightly golden. Remove it from the oven and immediately (but carefully) transfer it from the hot baking sheet to a cutting board or serving plate.

9. Eat it warm or at room temperature. Store leftovers in a resealable plastic bag for 1 or 2 days or freeze it for longer, then thaw and reheat to use.

NOTE *It's best to use a mix of all-purpose flour and high-protein or high-gluten flour. If you can't find the latter, substitute both with plain bread flour.*

FOCACCIA BARESE

Focaccia Bread with Tomatoes & Olives

This Apulian-style bread, from the city of Bari, is the quintessential southern Italian focaccia. It's characterized by a flavorful topping of tomatoes, olives, and oregano. This focaccia blends the line between pizza and bread, and should really be eaten hot and fresh for the best results. In Bari, they eat this focaccia any time of day, from breakfast to a midnight snack.

DURATION: 3 to 4 hours, largely unattended

YIELD: 8 servings

6 cups (720 g) bread flour

2 teaspoons (8 g) active dry yeast

1½ cups (360 ml) room-temperature water

4 teaspoons (20 g) salt

Pinch of granulated sugar

2 teaspoons (10 ml) extra-virgin olive oil, plus more for greasing and drizzling

14 ounces (400 g) canned whole peeled tomatoes, crushed with a fork or by hand

About 20 cherry tomatoes, cut in half

About 30 pitted Kalamata olives

Dried oregano

1. In a large bowl, thoroughly mix the flour and yeast by hand or with a wooden spoon. Add the water and mix with a wooden spoon until all the water is absorbed and a rough, crumbly dough forms. Add the salt, sugar, and ¼ cup (60 ml) of water and mix until all the ingredients are well incorporated.

2. Add the olive oil and mix it thoroughly into the dough; at this point, it will likely be more convenient to fold the dough by hand rather than mix it with the spoon. Cover the bowl with a lid or plastic wrap and let rest at room temperature for 20 minutes.

3. Slide your hand underneath the dough, along the side of the bowl, then lift and fold the edges of the dough into itself. Repeat this process, turning the bowl as you go to fold all the sides in. After folding in the edges, scoop the dough from the bottom with one hand and lift it out of the bowl. The ends should sag down around your hand. Place the dough back into the bowl so that the sags fold in beneath the dough ball. (In practice, this move looks like you are lifting the dough and setting it right back down again; it seems minor, but it helps to incorporate air into the dough.) Repeat this process 8 to 10 times, turning the bowl to "fold" it in slightly different directions. Cover the bowl again and let rest for 1½ hours, or until it has roughly doubled in size. (It's best to rest the dough in a warm place, such as an oven with the light on.)

continued on following page >>

4. Liberally grease the bottom and sides of a large, rimmed nonstick baking sheet (13 × 18 inches, or 33 × 46 cm, or similar) with olive oil. Place the risen dough in the prepared baking sheet and gently press it out with your fingertips, working from the center toward the edges. Spread the dough until it completely fills the baking sheet up to the edges. If the dough tends to shrink back from the corners, wait 10 minutes for the gluten to relax and try again.

5. Liberally drizzle the top of the dough with olive oil. Evenly spread the crushed tomatoes on top. (This is not a pizza, so there's no need to cover the whole surface; the tomatoes should just "dirty" the top.) Evenly arrange the cherry tomatoes over the focaccia, with the cut sides gently pressed into the dough. Spread the olives on top, then sprinkle with oregano.

6. Let the dough rise for 1 hour, or until it rises to reach the top edges of the baking sheet. Meanwhile, preheat the oven to 450°F (230°C).

7. Bake for 14 to 16 minutes, until the bottom is golden (you can carefully check it by lifting with a spatula) and the tomatoes are no longer wet. Carefully slide the focaccia onto a cutting board.

8. Serve hot, if possible, but it is also great at room temperature or reheated in a warm oven. The focaccia will last a day at room temperature, but it is best eaten as fresh as possible.

SFINCIONE PALERMITANO

Sicilian Thick-Crust Pizza

This thick Sicilian sfincione is possibly the ancestor of Detroit-style pizza. It has an incredible crust of spongy dough that beautifully soaks up the rich, savory sauce. It also has an advantage over Neapolitan pizza in that the dough can be made and cooked all in the same day. You might be tempted to skip the anchovies, but we highly recommend giving them a shot. The sauce packs a flavorful punch, and the anchovies add a zing of salty umami that is truly necessary to bring everything together. It won't taste fishy; we promise.

DURATION: 5 to 7 hours, largely unattended

YIELD: 6 to 8 servings

Dough

1 teaspoon (5 g) active dry yeast

1¼ cups (300 ml) room-temperature water

2½ cups (300 g) all-purpose flour, plus more for dusting

1⅔ cups (200 g) semolina flour, plus more for dusting

3½ teaspoons (15 g) granulated sugar

2 tablespoons (30 ml) extra-virgin olive oil, plus more for greasing drizzling and brushing

2½ teaspoons (12 g) salt

1. **To make the dough:** In a small bowl, stir the yeast with the water until it has dissolved. In a large bowl, combine the flours, sugar, 2 tablespoons (30 ml) olive oil, and 2½ teaspoons (12 g) salt. Mix everything together well, then gradually add the water with the yeast while continuing to mix by hand.

2. When all the water is incorporated and a rough dough has formed, transfer it to a clean work surface and knead until it is even and fairly smooth, 10 to 15 minutes. If the dough is sticky, dust it with a little semolina flour. (It should be soft and pliable; if it is too dry, you can work in a little more water.)

3. Place the finished dough back into the bowl, cover the bowl with plastic wrap, and let the dough rise at room temperature for 3 to 4 hours, until it roughly doubles in size.

4. Liberally brush a medium, rimmed nonstick baking sheet with olive oil and transfer the dough to the center. Rub a little oil on your fingers to prevent sticking and press the dough until it evenly fills the baking sheet into every corner. Cover with plastic wrap and let rise for 1 to 2 hours, until it is about 1 inch (2.5 cm) thick.

continued on following page >>

Tomato Sauce

¼ cup (60 ml) extra-virgin oil

2 large onions, thinly sliced

28 ounces (800 g) canned whole peeled tomatoes, crushed with a fork or by hand

Salt

Freshly ground black pepper

Toppings

About 10 anchovies, chopped

4 ounces (115 g) Sicilian caciocavallo cheese or sharp provolone, chopped

½ cup (45 g) bread crumbs, or to taste

Grated Sicilian caciocavallo cheese (see Note)

Dried oregano

5. While the dough rises, make the tomato sauce: In a large saucepan, combine the ¼ cup (60 ml) olive oil and onions over medium heat and cook, stirring frequently, until slightly tender, about 10 minutes.

6. Pour the tomatoes (plus all the puree from the can) into the pan. Stir everything together, season with a generous pinch each of salt and pepper, and bring to a gentle simmer. Let the sauce simmer, partially covered, for about 1 hour, or until the onions become very tender and the sauce thickens. Season again with salt as the sauce nears completion, then remove from the heat.

7. When the dough has risen, preheat the oven to 410°F (210°C). Sprinkle the anchovies and chopped cheese evenly over the dough, then spread the tomato sauce in a thick layer all over.

8. Bake for 20 minutes, then remove the pizza from the oven and reduce the temperature to 400°F (205°C). Sprinkle the top with bread crumbs, a generous grating of cheese, and dried oregano. Bake for an additional 10 minutes, or until the cheese is melted and beginning to crisp.

9. Serve warm and fresh for best results, but sfincione is also delicious at room temperature.

NOTE *If you can't find Sicilian caciocavallo, you can substitute it with pecorino or Parmigiano-Reggiano.*

PIZZA ALLA NAPOLETANA

⇥ *Neapolitan Margherita Pizza* ⇤

The biggest challenge with making real Neapolitan-style pizza at home is achieving a suitable oven temperature. A wood pizza oven reaches temperatures of about 900°F (485°C), and a pizza can cook in it in around 90 seconds. The longer the cook time, the denser and chewier the dough will be. The usual home solution—a pizza stone or steel—makes the best of a poor situation. In order to pull off the best pizza possible in a normal oven, the dough must be highly hydrated, as in the case of this recipe (75 percent hydration). For this reason, it's critical that you do not, under any circumstances, add more flour to the recipe (no matter how sticky the dough feels). This recipe will work even better in the increasingly popular home pizza ovens which do, in fact, reach Neapolitan oven temperatures.

Making pizza is one rare case in Italian cuisine in which precision is paramount. The ingredients must be measured by weight, not by volume, in order to achieve the correct ratios.

DURATION: Up to 24 hours, largely unattended

YIELD: 5 pizzas (12 inches, or 30 cm, each)

Dough

500 grams high-protein pizza flour (see Note on page 73), plus more for dusting

2 grams active dry yeast

375 milliliters water, divided

10 grams salt

About 2 cups (240 g) semolina flour, for dusting

1. To make the dough: In a large bowl, thoroughly mix the flour and yeast. Add 250 milliliters of the water and mix it into the flour with a wooden spoon until a rough dough forms. Dissolve the salt in the remaining 125 milliliters water, then mix this into the dough. Once all the flour is wet (it's okay if the dough is sticky and not smooth), cover the bowl with a lid or plastic wrap and let rest at room temperature for 30 minutes.

2. Liberally wet your hands with water. Slide your hand underneath the dough, along the side of the bowl, then lift and fold the edge of the dough into itself. Repeat this process, turning the bowl as you go to fold all the sides in. (Don't worry if the dough is very sticky; this is a good thing—just be sure to keep your hand wet.) After folding in the edges, scoop the dough from the bottom with one hand and lift it out of the bowl. The ends should sag down around your hand. Place the dough back into the bowl so that the sags fold in beneath the dough ball. (In practice, this move looks like you are lifting the dough up and setting it right back down again; it seems minor, but it helps to incorporate air into the dough.) Repeat this process 8 to 10 times, turning the bowl to "fold" it in slightly different directions. Cover the bowl again and let the dough rest for an additional 30 minutes.

3. After 30 minutes, the dough should look significantly smoother. Repeat the above step, folding the edges in, then performing the "lift" move 8 to 10 times. During the latter procedure, feel free to gently shake the dough as you lift it so that it sags down farther and creates a deeper fold. Cover the bowl and let the dough rest for an additional 30 minutes

Tomato Sauce

⅔ cup (160 ml) tomato passata (puree)

1 tablespoon (15 ml) extra-virgin olive oil

Salt

Toppings

About 10½ ounces (300 g) fresh mozzarella cheese, chopped or shredded by hand

About 25 fresh basil leaves

Extra-virgin olive oil, for drizzling

4. Wet your hands and a large work surface with water; the surface can be a very large cutting board or smooth counter/table, but the whole surface should have a visible amount of water covering it. Place the dough on the center of the wet surface. Using your (wet) hands, stretch the dough into a big square, about 20 inches (50 cm) per side. (Don't be afraid to stretch it out with some force; if you are using a good flour, the dough can take some abuse.) Fold each corner of the dough into the center, then repeat with the newly formed corners of the resulting smaller square. Repeat one more time to fold the dough into a big ball of folded dough. Flip the dough ball over so the smooth side is on top.

5. Place the dough on the farthest side of the work surface from you, gently cup your hands around it, then drag the ball toward you; the friction on the wet surface will pull the opposite edge underneath the bottom and make the top even smoother. Rotate the dough 90 degrees and repeat. Continue to repeat this process a few more times until the dough ball is very smooth and uniform on top. Place the dough back in the bowl, cover it again, and let rest for 1½ hours.

6. Place the bowl in the refrigerator and let the dough rest for 16 to 18 hours. A low-protein flour will not work with a long rest time in the fridge, so this is where the ingredient quality becomes critical.

7. Start checking the dough after 12 hours. If at some point the dough becomes extremely bubbly and rises a lot (this is a good sign), simply repeat step 2 and lift/fold the dough to release some air before continuing the refrigerated rest of 16 to 18 hours. Skip this step if you are within 2 hours of removing the dough from the fridge.

8. Remove the dough from the fridge and let come to room temperature for 1 hour.

9. Lightly dust a large baking sheet, a work surface, and your hands with semolina flour. Transfer the dough to the work surface and cut it into 5 equal portions (you can use a scale if you like; each piece should be about 170 grams). Take one portion in your hands and gently pull and tuck the edges underneath the ball; the resulting effect should be similar to the dragging method and will form a smooth top. Place the ball on the baking sheet and repeat with the other dough portions. Lightly dust the dough balls with pizza flour, loosely cover the baking sheet with plastic wrap, and let the dough rest until the balls have noticeably risen (1 to 2 hours, depending on the temperature).

10. Preheat the oven with a pizza stone inside at maximum temperature for at least 1 hour.

continued on page 73 >>

11. Meanwhile, make the tomato sauce: In a small bowl, mix together the tomato passata and olive oil. Season with salt.

12. Place the semolina flour into a flattened pile on a large work surface. Scoop up a dough ball and place it upside down into the flour (a large, clean, kitchen-only painting scraper is an excellent tool for this). Flip the dough back over so that both sides are dusted in flour, keeping the dough in the flour pile. Working from the center out, gently press your fingers into the dough and push it out toward the edges to spread the dough. Do not touch the edges, as you want a nice, bubbly crust there!

13. Once the dough begins to spread out a bit, lift it out of the flour and place on a clean (not floured) surface to keep spreading. You can also gently lift the dough (again, don't press the edges while you do so) and carefully stretch it to add some additional size. (This takes practice; Neapolitan pizza chefs spend years learning to do this, so be patient!)

14. Once the pizza is about 10 inches (25 cm) in diameter, use a spoon to spread an even layer of tomato sauce over the pizza, leaving the crust bare. Place a large pizza peel right next to the dough and flush with the surface (having an assistant hold it is helpful). Carefully grasp the edges of the dough and drag it onto the peel. (It will seem scary at first, but you will be amazed at how easy it is to do.) Once the pizza is on the peel, grasp the dough (again, do not crimp the edges!) and gently stretch them in opposing directions until the pizza is 12 inches (30 cm) in diameter.

15. Hover the pizza peel over the hot pizza stone and, with a quick pulling motion, slide the pizza onto the stone. Close the oven and keep a close eye on the pizza. Once the crust has fully puffed up, pull the oven rack out and add some chopped mozzarella (about 2 ounces, or 60 g, per pizza, or to taste) 4 or 5 basil leaves, and a drizzle of olive oil. Close the oven door and cook the pizza until the crust begins to brown and the cheese has melted. The cook time will vary, depending on how hot your oven can get, and you may find that you need to rotate it if it cooks unevenly. The pizza can be manipulated by pulling it back onto the peel with a fork and turning it as needed. Serve immediately. Repeat steps 12 to 15 to cook the remaining pizzas.

NOTE *The biggest problem we see with home cooks struggling to make a good dough is the use of poor-quality or unsuitable flour. Excellent pizza requires "00" flour with a protein content of at least 12.5 percent (although preferably even higher, in the 14 to 15 percent range). Many manufacturers label their flour in tricky ways, so don't be fooled by any old "pizza flour." If you're looking for a specific recommendation, check out Caputo Pizzeria Flour, which is widely available online and in specialty shops.*

PIZZA TOPPINGS

There's a myth that Italians have some sort of "rule" that a pizza can't have more than two or three toppings. The only rule is that they should be good toppings that work well together. Here is a brief list of some common pizza styles you'll find in most Italian pizzerias and can try at home.

Remember that tomato sauce for pizza should always be raw, never precooked (see step 11 for Pizza alla Napoletana on page 73).

Marinara: Tomato sauce, anchovies, dried oregano, and olive oil.

Caprese: The pizza dough is cooked white, without any toppings. After cooking, the following is added raw: chopped tomatoes (cherry tomatoes are great), mozzarella, basil, olive oil, and freshly ground black pepper (optional).

Quattro Stagioni (Four Seasons): This pizza is divided into quarters, all with a base of tomato sauce, mozzarella cheese, a drizzle of olive oil, and one of the following ingredients: artichoke hearts, black olives, sautéed mushrooms, or prosciutto cotto (ham).

Tonno e Cipolla: Tomato sauce, canned tuna fish, sliced sweet onion, and olive oil.

Diavola: Tomato sauce, spicy salami, mozzarella, and olive oil.

Quattro Formaggi (Four Cheese): Mozzarella, Gorgonzola, Fontina, Parmigiano-Reggiano, and olive oil (no tomato sauce!).

San Daniele: Tomato sauce, basil, mozzarella, olive oil, and thinly sliced prosciutto crudo—the prosciutto is added right after the pizza comes out of the oven.

Vegetariana: Tomato sauce, grilled vegetables (such as eggplant, zucchini, and bell peppers), olive oil, and mozzarella (optional).

Americana: Tomato sauce, basil, mozzarella, sliced hot dogs, and french fries—the french fries are added right after the pizza comes out of the oven (yes, this is real and delicious).

CALZONE

⇥ *Stuffed Pizza* ⇤

A calzone is simply a pizza that is stuffed instead of topped. The fillings have just as much variety as pizza toppings, but one of the most classic is mozzarella cheese and prosciutto cotto (ham). The dough is the same as Pizza alla Napoletana (page 70), so follow the steps in that recipe up until the stretching of the dough. This recipe uses a pizza stone or steel, so be sure to preheat the stone at the maximum oven temperature for at least an hour, just like with a pizza.

DURATION: 45 minutes

YIELD: 5 calzoni

Pizza alla Napoletana dough (page 70)

10½ ounces (300 g) mozzarella cheese, chopped

10 slices prosciutto cotto or ham, shredded or chopped into small pieces

Salt

Extra-virgin olive oil, for drizzling

5 tablespoons (75 ml) tomato passata (puree)

1. Preheat the oven with a pizza stone inside at maximum temperature for at least 1 hour.

2. Spread out the pizza dough just like you would with a pizza, but this time you can press and spread it right up to the edges. Try to stretch the dough out a little bit wider, to about 12 inches (30 cm) in diameter.

3. Spread the mozzarella and ham over half of the pizza dough, leaving about 1 inch (2.5 cm) of dough bare around the edge. Sprinkle the stuffing with a pinch of salt, and drizzle with olive oil.

4. Fold the bare half of the pizza dough over the stuffing and pinch the edges closed so that the calzone is completely sealed. Brush the top of the calzone with a thin layer of tomato passata and carefully transfer it onto a pizza peel.

5. Hover the peel over the hot pizza stone and, with a quick pulling motion, slide the calzone onto the stone. Close the oven and keep a close eye on the calzone as the cook time will vary depending on the temperature of the oven. When the top crust begins to brown, remove the calzone with the pizza peel.

6. Serve immediately. Repeat the steps above to make the remaining calzoni.

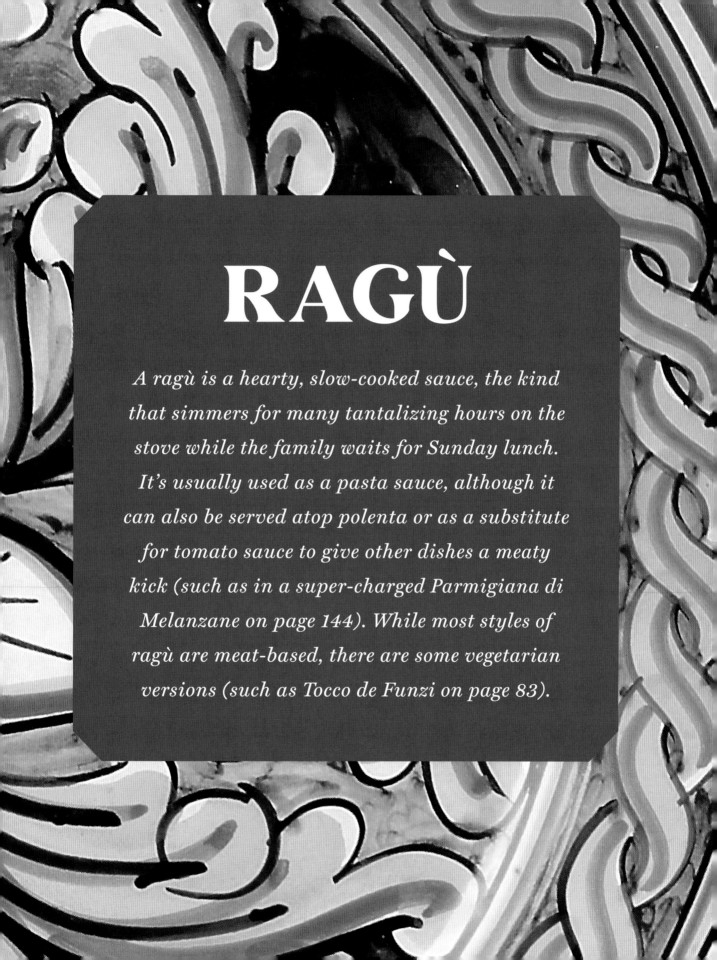

RAGÙ

A ragù is a hearty, slow-cooked sauce, the kind that simmers for many tantalizing hours on the stove while the family waits for Sunday lunch. It's usually used as a pasta sauce, although it can also be served atop polenta or as a substitute for tomato sauce to give other dishes a meaty kick (such as in a super-charged Parmigiana di Melanzane on page 144). While most styles of ragù are meat-based, there are some vegetarian versions (such as Tocco de Funzi on page 83).

RAGÙ ALLA BOLOGNESE

⇥ *Minced Meat Ragù* ⇤

This classic ragù is the perfect sauce for fresh egg pasta, such as tagliatelle (see How to Make Fresh Egg Pasta on page 22) and is also the base of Lasagna alla Bolognese (page 120). In short, it's a versatile recipe to have up your sleeve. You can make a large batch and freeze it in portions to thaw for a quick and delicious pasta dinner. Originally, ragù alla Bolognese was cooked with no (or very little) tomato. Even today in Bologna, adding tomatoes to ragù is controversial, with many purists using just a little bit of tomato paste, at most. In this case, the result is more of a meat mince than what many of us would recognize as a "sauce." However, more and more Bolognese cooks are acquiescing to the almighty passata, and we have to admit that we agree with the more modern approach, if only because the extra liquid is crucial for making an excellent lasagna. If you want a more traditional ragù, skip the whole peeled tomatoes and add a little water as necessary to keep the meat moist while it cooks.

DURATION: 3 to 4 hours, largely unattended

YIELD: About 5 cups (a little over 1 L)

———————————

5 tablespoons (75 ml) extra-virgin olive oil

¼ large carrot, diced

¼ large onion, diced

1 rib celery, diced

2 slices (20 g) pancetta (or bacon), diced

1 pound (450 g) ground beef

1 pound (450 g) ground pork

Pinch of ground nutmeg

Salt and freshly ground black pepper

1 cup (240 ml) white or red wine

2 tablespoons (30 g) tomato paste

28 ounces (800 g) canned whole peeled tomatoes, crushed with a fork or by hand

1. In a large, heavy pot (preferably terra-cotta or a Dutch oven), heat the olive oil over medium heat. Add the carrot, onion, and celery and cook, stirring frequently, for 5 to 7 minutes, until the onion is tender and slightly transparent. Stir in the bacon and cook for 3 more minutes.

2. Add the ground meat and cook until browned, breaking it up into a fine crumble with a wooden spoon as it cooks. (Depending on the meat you use, you may find that a lot of water is released; bring the mince to a brisk simmer and, stirring frequently, let the excess liquid burn off.) When browned, add the nutmeg and a generous sprinkle of salt and pepper.

3. Pour in the wine, bring the ragù to a simmer, and cook until the smell of alcohol has dissipated. Stir in the tomato paste. Continue to simmer the sauce for 3 minutes, then add the crushed tomatoes and ½ cup (120 ml) of water. Season with a generous sprinkle of salt.

4. Bring the sauce to a gentle simmer, then partially cover the pot. Let the sauce cook for 2½ to 3 hours minimum, stirring and checking on the ragù every 10 minutes or so. (You can always increase the cook time for extra flavor-building.) The finished ragù should resemble a thick chili. If, at any time, it thickens too much, add a little warm water to thin it out again. As the ragù nears completion, be sure to taste it and add salt as necessary.

5. Use right away or refrigerate in an airtight container for up to 3 days. The ragù can be frozen for up to 3 months and reheated in a pot after thawing.

RAGÙ ALLA GENOVESE

⤚ *Beef & Onion Ragù* ⤙

Despite the name, this ragù did not originate in Genoa but in Naples. One theory behind the title is that it was popular among Genoese sailors who visited the Campania city. Ragù alla Genovese is a very slow cook but well worth the effort. You need a ton of onions, which reduce into a creamy, hearty sauce. It's a favorite among guests who travel with us to Naples on the Pasta Grammar Tour. The ragù itself can be served as a pasta sauce (we recommend rigatoni, candele, penne lisce, or other tube-shaped pasta) for a first course, and the remaining beef can be served as a second course (topped with some of the leftover ragù, of course).

DURATION: 10 hours, largely unattended

YIELD: 8 to 10 servings

½ cup (120 ml) extra-virgin olive oil

3 tablespoons (40 g) lard

3½ pounds (1.5 kg) lean beef steak, cut into roughly 4-inch (10 cm) chunks

½ large carrot, diced

1 rib celery, diced

4 bay leaves

1 cup (240 ml) white wine

6½ pounds (3 kg) onions, sliced

1 tablespoon (15 g) tomato paste

Salt and freshly ground black pepper

1. In a large, heavy pot (preferably terra-cotta or a Dutch oven), heat the olive oil and lard over medium heat. Add the meat chunks and brown them on all sides. If the meat releases a lot of water, just let it simmer off, at which point the beef will begin to brown. Add the carrot, celery, and bay leaves and cook, stirring frequently, for 2 to 3 minutes.

2. Add the wine and bring it to a brisk simmer. Let simmer until most of the liquid has evaporated, then stir in the onions and cover the pot with the lid. (If the onions overfill the pot, press them in, then cover the pot.) Reduce the heat to medium-low and let steam for 10 to 15 minutes, until the onions wilt and lose volume.

3. Add a generous pinch of salt and stir everything together. Reduce the heat to low, partially cover the pot, and let the ragù cook, stirring occasionally, for 1 hour, or until the onions are extremely tender and have released a lot of liquid.

4. Stir in the tomato paste, partially cover the pot again, and let cook for 7 to 9 hours, until the onions have transformed into an almost creamy sauce. As the sauce nears completion, season with salt and pepper.

5. Ladle out the sauce to mix with pasta as a first course, then keep the beef chunks warm in the sauce and serve separately as a second course.

RAGÙ ALLA NAPOLETANA

↤ *Neapolitan-Style Meat Ragù* ↦

This is truly a special occasion dish, usually reserved for large family Sunday lunch gatherings and holidays. Neapolitan ragù is special for a number of reasons: it's incredibly rich and delicious, it takes a long time to make, and it provides the sauce for a first course of pasta and the meat for a second course, at the same time. We recommend pairing the ragù with fresh egg ribbon pasta, such as tagliatelle (see How to Make Fresh Egg Pasta on page 22). The meat used can vary quite a lot, sometimes including meatballs (see Polpette al Sugo on page 149) or Braciole (page 153). What's important is that you have a good mix of fatty pork and beef in large pieces. It is always removed and served separately, while the sauce can be paired with pasta or used in a lasagna.

DURATION: 5 to 6 hours, largely unattended

YIELD: About 5 cups (a little over 1 L) of ragù, plus meat for a second course; 6 to 8 servings

¼ cup (55 g) pork lard

1 large whole Italian sausage

6 pork spareribs

10 ounces (285 g) pork belly, cut into 2 or 3 large chunks

1 pound (450 g) beef chuck roast, cut into 3 or 4 large chunks

½ large onion, diced

1 rib celery, diced

½ large carrot, diced

6 to 8 fresh basil leaves

Salt and freshly ground black pepper

1½ cups (360 ml) red wine

3 tablespoons (45 g) tomato paste

56 ounces (1.6 L) tomato passata (puree)

1 cup (240 ml) warm water

1. In a large, heavy pot (preferably terra-cotta or a Dutch oven), melt the lard over medium-high heat. Pierce the sausage in a few places with the tip of a sharp paring knife, then add all the meat. (Don't be afraid to crowd the pot.) Turning and mixing the pieces often, cook the meat until it is browned on all sides. If the meat releases a lot of water, just give it time to boil off, at which point the meat will brown properly.

2. Add the onion, celery, carrot, and basil. Season with salt and pepper and cook until the onion is tender, 2 to 3 minutes. Add the wine and let simmer for 30 minutes.

3. Stir in the tomato paste, tomato passata, and warm water. Add a generous pinch or two of salt, then partially cover the pot and bring the ragù to a gentle simmer. Cook for 2 to 3 hours, stirring occasionally, until the meat is very tender and almost falling off the bone.

4. Using tongs, remove the meat from the sauce and set it aside. Bring the sauce to a simmer again, partially covered, and cook for an additional 1 to 2 hours. You can always add warm water and continue to cook for even longer, developing the flavors further. As the ragù nears completion, taste it and add salt as necessary.

5. If you plan on serving the ragù with pasta as the first course and the meat as a second course, place the meat back into the finished sauce over low heat so that it can reheat and stay moist. Cook and drain your pasta as directed. Place the pasta back in its pot and ladle in enough ragù to fully coat it. Stir over medium-high heat for 1 to 2 minutes. Serve immediately, topped with extra ragù and grated Parmigiano or pecorino cheese. Keep the meat warm in the sauce until everyone has finished the first course, then serve it.

SUGO DI SPUNTATURE E SALSICCE

⤜ *Pork Ribs & Sausage Ragù* ⤛

This style of ragù hails from Abruzzo, where it is typically served atop polenta instead of pasta. That being said, it can easily be used in the same manner as Ragù alla Napoletana (page 81), in which the resulting sauce is used for fresh pasta as a first course, and the meat follows as a second course.

DURATION: 2½ hours, largely unattended

YIELD: About 5 cups (a little over 1 L) of ragù, plus meat for a second course; 6 to 8 servings

¼ cup lard (50 g) or extra-virgin olive oil (60 ml)

8 pork spareribs

4 whole Italian sausages

¼ large onion, diced

1 rib celery, diced

½ large carrot, diced

Salt and freshly ground black pepper

1 cup (240 ml) red wine

About 5 fresh basil leaves, torn

56 ounces (1.6 L) tomato passata (puree)

2 tablespoons (30 g) tomato paste

1. Heat the lard in a large, heavy pot (preferably terra-cotta or a Dutch oven) over medium-high heat. Add the ribs and sausages and shallow-fry them until they are lightly browned on all sides. Pierce the sausages with the point of a sharp knife as they cook to prevent bursting. If the meat releases a lot of water, just give it time to boil off, at which point the meat will brown properly.

2. Add the onion, celery, and carrot and cook, stirring frequently, until the onion is tender and slightly transparent, 2 to 3 minutes. Sprinkle the meat with a pinch each of salt and pepper.

3. Add the wine and basil, reduce the heat to medium-low, and bring the liquid to a simmer. Let the wine reduce for about 15 minutes, partially covered.

4. Add the tomato passata, tomato paste, and ⅓ cup (80 ml) of water. Bring the ragù to a simmer again and lightly season it with salt (the flavor will concentrate as the sauce cooks, so go easy on the seasoning at this point). Let the ragù simmer, stirring occasionally, for about 2 hours, or until the meat is very tender. Remove the meat from the sauce using tongs and set it aside. At this point, you can leave the ragù as it is, or continue to reduce it if you prefer a thicker sauce.

5. Serve hot, drizzled on top of polenta, or use it as a pasta sauce. The meat can be reheated in the leftover ragù and served as a second course. To serve with pasta, cook and drain the pasta as directed. Place the pasta back in its pot and ladle in enough ragù to fully coat it. Stir over medium-high heat for 1 to 2 minutes. Serve immediately, topped with extra ragù and grated Parmigiano or pecorino cheese. Keep the meat warm in the sauce until everyone has finished the first course, then serve it.

TOCCO DE FUNZI

⤙ *Vegetarian Mushroom Ragù* ⤚

In general, the term *ragù* implies a hearty meat sauce. But that's not always the case, as evidenced by this vegetarian mushroom ragù from Liguria. While it's normally served with fresh egg pasta (substitute rigatoni for a vegan version), we've come to love this sauce so much, we use it in a few different ways. One of our favorites is to use it as the sauce base for poached eggs (a dish called "shakshuka" in North Africa and the Middle East).

DURATION: 2 hours, largely unattended

YIELD: 4 servings

1¾ ounces (50 g) dried mushrooms (preferably porcini, but you can substitute with another variety of choice)

¼ cup (60 ml) extra-virgin olive oil

1 clove garlic, diced

2 shallots or ¼ large onion, diced

1 teaspoon (2 g) chopped fresh rosemary, or to taste

¾ cup (180 ml) white wine

1½ tablespoons (23 g) tomato paste

1¾ cups (420 ml) tomato passata (puree)

Salt and freshly ground black pepper

4 servings fresh pappardelle (see How to Make Fresh Egg Pasta on page 22)

Grated Parmigiano-Reggiano or pecorino cheese, for topping (optional)

1. Soak the dried mushrooms in a small bowl of water for 1 hour. Remove a handful of them, reserving the rest. Squeeze out the excess water and chop them.

2. In a large pot, combine the chopped mushrooms with the olive oil, garlic, shallots, and rosemary over medium heat and cook, stirring frequently, until the shallots are tender and slightly transparent, 2 to 3 minutes.

3. Remove the reserved mushrooms from the soaking water, reserving the soaking water. Squeeze out the excess moisture and add the mushrooms, whole, to the pot. Cook, stirring frequently, for 1 to 2 minutes, then add the wine and bring the sauce to a simmer. Cook for 2 to 3 minutes, until the smell of alcohol has dissipated.

4. Meanwhile, dissolve the tomato paste in 1 cup (240 ml) of the reserved mushroom soaking water. When the alcohol from the wine has cooked off, add the tomato passata and diluted tomato paste to the pot. Bring to a simmer and season with a pinch of salt and plenty of black pepper.

5. Partially cover the pot and let the ragù cook, stirring occasionally, for at least 45 minutes (the longer, the better). If the sauce thickens too much, add a little bit of the reserved soaking water as needed to maintain moisture. Allow the sauce to thicken as it nears completion and season it again with salt.

6. To serve with pasta, ladle plenty of ragù into a large pan. Cook the fresh pasta as directed (see How to Cook Pasta on page 27), then use tongs to transfer it to the pan with the ragù. Stir together over medium-high heat until the pasta is completely coated in sauce. You can always add more ragù from the pot if desired.

7. Serve immediately, topped with some extra sauce and a grating of Parmigiano-Reggiano or pecorino (if using).

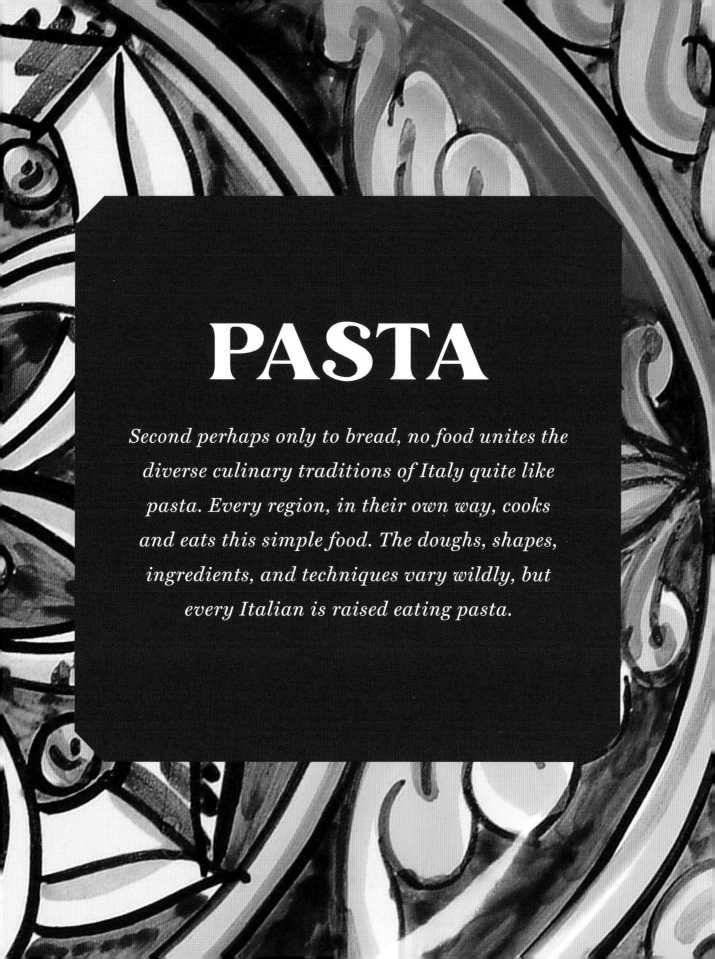

PASTA

Second perhaps only to bread, no food unites the diverse culinary traditions of Italy quite like pasta. Every region, in their own way, cooks and eats this simple food. The doughs, shapes, ingredients, and techniques vary wildly, but every Italian is raised eating pasta.

PASTA ALLA PUTTANESCA

⇥ *Pasta with Anchovies, Capers, Olives & Tomatoes* ⇤

The name of this classic dish literally translates to "prostitute-style pasta." Many theories have been proposed about where the name comes from, none being particularly convincing. All we know for sure is that it's a yummy recipe and one that every pasta lover should try at some point. The anchovies naturally bring salt into the sauce, so you generally don't need to season it further. Taste the sauce as it cooks and add salt if necessary, but be careful not to accidentally overdo it.

DURATION: 20 minutes

YIELD: 3 or 4 servings

3 tablespoons (45 ml) extra-virgin olive oil

1 clove garlic, crushed with the skin on

4 anchovies (in oil)

15 to 20 pitted Kalamata olives, chopped

2 tablespoons (24 g) capers, diced

14 ounces (400 g) canned whole peeled tomatoes, crushed with a fork or by hand

Salt

12 ounces (340 g) spaghetti or linguine

Chopped fresh parsley, for topping

1. Put a large pot of water on to boil. While the water comes up to temperature, begin cooking the sauce.

2. In a large pan, heat the olive oil and garlic over medium heat. When the garlic starts to sizzle, remove and discard it. Reduce the heat to low and add the anchovies. Stir until they completely dissolve in the oil, then increase the heat to medium again.

3. Add the olives and capers to the pan and cook, stirring frequently, for 1 minute. Add the crushed tomatoes, bring the sauce to a simmer, and season with salt. Let the sauce simmer, stirring occasionally, for at least 5 minutes, or until it thickens slightly. Turn off the heat while the pasta cooks.

4. When the water comes to a rolling boil, salt it generously and add the pasta. Cook it for 2 to 3 minutes less than the recommended al dente cook time on the package.

5. Use tongs or a pasta fork to transfer the cooked pasta to the tomato sauce, along with a few spoonfuls of pasta water. Stir everything together over high heat until the excess liquid has thickened and the pasta is al dente to your taste. If the sauce thickens too quickly or too much, thin it with some more pasta water.

6. Serve immediately topped with chopped parsley.

BUSIATE CON PESTO ALLA TRAPANESE

Sicilian Pesto Pasta

While the understanding of the word "pesto" is dominated by the Genovese version (see Trenette al Pesto on page 102), there are actually many kinds in Italy. In Trapani, Sicily, they make this tomato-based version and serve it with busiate pasta. Like pesto alla Genovese, it's best made with a very large mortar and pestle. If you don't have one, you can use a blender, but only do so by pulsing the machine so as not to overheat and cook the ingredients.

DURATION: 45 minutes

YIELD: 3 or 4 servings

½ cup (60 g) whole almonds

10 ounces (285 g) cherry or grape tomatoes

4 cloves garlic, chopped

Coarse sea salt

About 20 fresh basil leaves

2 ounces (60 g) pecorino cheese, or to taste, grated, plus more for topping

2 tablespoons (30 g) extra-virgin olive oil, or to taste, plus more for drizzling

12 ounces (340 g) busiate

1. Preheat the oven to 350°F (175°C). Put a small pot of water on to boil.

2. Place the almonds in a small, rimmed baking sheet and roast them in the oven for 10 minutes.

3. Meanwhile use a paring knife to cut a small incision across one end of each tomato. Drop the tomatoes into the boiling water, boil for 1 minute, and then drain them. Peel the tomato skins with a paring knife from the incisions you made earlier. Cut the tomatoes in half and scoop out and discard the seeds.

4. Finely chop the roasted almonds.

5. Place the garlic and a generous pinch of salt into the bowl of a large stone mortar and pestle (you can make the pesto in batches if using a smaller mortar and pestle bowl). With a circular grinding motion, mash the garlic into a paste. Add the basil and grind it into a paste (which can take some time, so be patient). Add the tomatoes and grind them into pulp. When a salsa-like sauce has formed, add the chopped almonds and pecorino and grind them into a thick paste. If there is a lot of liquid in the pesto from the tomatoes, skim some of it out with a spoon and discard it. Mix in the olive oil. Taste the pesto and add more salt, cheese, and/or olive oil as desired.

6. Bring a large pot of water to a boil and salt it generously. Add the pasta and cook according to the package directions until al dente to your taste. Meanwhile, place the pesto in a large bowl. Transfer the cooked pasta to the bowl using tongs and stir everything together. If the pesto is too thick to evenly coat the pasta, thin it with a few spoonfuls of pasta water.

7. Serve immediately topped with a drizzle of olive oil and some more grated pecorino.

PASTA E FAGIOLI

⇥ *Calabrian-Style Pasta with Beans* ⇤

While pasta fazool is most commonly recognized in its soupiest form, this Calabrian version of pasta with beans needs no spoon to be eaten. It's thick, hearty, spicy, and one of our favorite dishes to serve to guests who visit us in Dasà. One of the best features of this dish is the refried leftovers. Heat a generous amount of olive oil in a large pan and refry the cold leftovers until they become slightly crispy.

DURATION: 2½ hours, largely unattended

YIELD: 3 or 4 servings

—————————————

5½ ounces (160 g) dried cannellini beans

Salt

2 cloves garlic, peeled, divided

1 whole dried chili pepper

¼ cup (60 ml) extra-virgin olive oil, plus more for drizzling

½ cup (120 ml) tomato passata (puree)

Freshly ground black pepper

12 ounces (340 g) fileja (see Note)

Calabrian chili powder, for topping (optional)

1. Place the dried beans in a small pot and fill with water to cover them. Bring to simmer over medium-low heat and cook for 2 hours, or until the beans are soft but not mushy; stir the beans occasionally by swirling the pot, but never stir them with a utensil. Add hot water as necessary to keep the beans covered. As the beans near completion, add salt to taste, 1 garlic clove, and the chili pepper and mix them in by swirling. Turn off the heat when the beans are fully cooked.

2. Put a large pot of water on to boil for the pasta and salt it generously. While the water comes up to temperature, heat the olive oil and remaining garlic clove in a large pan over medium heat until the garlic starts to sizzle. Ladle in the cooked beans and enough of the bean soaking water to cover the beans. Reserve the remaining bean soaking water for later. Bring the beans to a simmer over medium heat.

3. Add the tomato passata to the pan and let the sauce simmer while the pasta cooks. Season with salt and black pepper.

4. When the pasta water comes to a rolling boil, add the pasta and cook as directed on the package until al dente to your taste. Drain the pasta fully and return it to the pot.

5. Remove the garlic clove from the sauce and discard it, then pour the sauce into the pasta pot. Stir everything together over medium-high heat until the pasta is completely coated in the sauce. If the sauce is too dry, thin it with some of the reserved bean cooking water and keep stirring over medium-high heat until creamy.

6. Serve immediately topped with a light dusting of chili powder (if using) and a drizzle of olive oil.

NOTE *The most traditional choice of pasta is fileja, sometimes known as "filei" by non-Calabrians. If you can't find it, try making it with casarecce, mezze maniche, or even bucatini (Mamma Rosa's shape of choice). You can even substitute boiled arborio rice for the pasta.*

CACIO E PEPE

⤙ *Cheese & Pepper Pasta* ⤚

This cheesy, Roman classic is an increasingly popular dish outside of the Eternal City. It's about as simple as a pasta dish can be but also a frustrating recipe, as creating a smooth pecorino cream without clumps can prove challenging. Many prominent cooks have devised "foolproof" methods, often resorting to blenders or xanthum gum, but these techniques miss the entire point of this dish: to be a quick and simple pasta that anyone can whip up at a moment's notice. The quality of the pecorino cheese and pasta (most Italians use tonnarelli, a fresh egg pasta that is difficult to make or find outside of Italy) play a part in making a creamy, smooth sauce. However, the following recipe will work perfectly with an average cheese and store-bought spaghetti. The secret is to let the cooked pasta cool before gradually adding the cheese.

DURATION: 30 minutes

YIELD: 3 or 4 servings

2 tablespoons (14 g) black peppercorns

Salt

12 ounces (340 g) spaghetti

7 ounces (200 g) pecorino cheese, grated (see Note)

1. Put a large pot of water on to boil. Meanwhile, toast the peppercorns in a large pan over medium-high heat for 4 minutes, or until you can smell the spice. Turn off the heat and transfer the peppercorns to a mortar and pestle. Coarsely grind them, then return the ground pepper to the pan.

2. When the pasta water comes to a rolling boil, salt it generously. Add the spaghetti and cook it for 3 minutes less than the recommended al dente cook time on the package. Add 1 or 2 ladlefuls of the pasta water to the pepper pan. Bring the sauce to a simmer and let it cook while the pasta boils. Add more pasta water to the pan as necessary to maintain a simmer.

3. When the pasta is 3 minutes from al dente, turn off the water heat, reserving the pasta water. Use tongs or a spaghetti fork to transfer the pasta into the pepper sauce. Add 2 or 3 more ladlefuls of pasta water to the pan, bring to a simmer while stirring over high heat, and then simmer and stir until the pasta is al dente to your taste, adding a little more water as needed to maintain moisture. Turn off the heat and let the pasta cool for 3 minutes.

4. Sprinkle a very light dusting of cheese over the pasta, add 1 or 2 small spoonfuls of pasta water, and stir vigorously until the cheese evenly melts. Do not add the cheese in thick clumps. Continue adding a little bit each of cheese and pasta water until all the cheese is melted. Serve immediately topped with a drizzle of the pan sauce and a grating of pecorino cheese, if desired.

NOTE *Many brands of pecorino outside of Italy lack flavor and can be too salty. If you don't have access to an excellent pecorino, use half pecorino and half Parmigiano-Reggiano.*

BUCATINI ALL'AMATRICIANA

Tomato & Guanciale Pasta

This is considered one of the classic Roman pasta dishes, despite conspicuously hailing from the nearby city of Amatrice. Bucatini is a bit of an odd duck in Italian cuisine. It's considered the most difficult shape of pasta to eat (without making a mess, that is) and is avoided by most Italians except in a handful of dishes in which, for some ineffable reason, it is the best choice. As the name suggests, bucatini all'Amatriciana is one of those dishes.

DURATION: 30 minutes

YIELD: 3 or 4 servings

---

5 ounces (140 g) guanciale, skin trimmed and cut into ½-inch (13 mm) cubes

⅔ cup (160 ml) white wine

28 ounces (800 g) canned whole peeled tomatoes, crushed with a fork

1 whole fresh chili pepper (optional)

Salt and freshly ground black pepper

12 ounces (340 g) bucatini

2 ounces (60 g) pecorino cheese, grated, plus more for topping

1. Put a large pot of water on to boil. While the water comes up to temperature, begin cooking the sauce.

2. In a large pan, cook the guanciale, stirring occasionally, over medium heat for 3 to 5 minutes, until the meat has released plenty of fat into the pan.

3. Add the wine, reduce the heat to medium-low, and bring to a gentle simmer. Cook until the smell of alcohol has dissipated, about 2 minutes. Add the tomatoes and chili pepper (if using) and season with salt and black pepper. Let simmer for 12 to 14 minutes, until the sauce thickens. (Turn off the heat if the pasta needs more time to cook.)

4. Meanwhile, salt the boiling water generously and add the pasta. Cook as directed on the package until al dente to taste.

5. Use tongs to transfer the cooked bucatini to the sauce. Stir everything together over medium-high heat until the pasta is completely coated in sauce. Turn off the heat and stir in the pecorino.

6. Serve immediately topped with extra cheese.

ORECCHIETTE ALLE CIME DI RAPA

⇥ *Pasta with Broccoli Rabe* ⇤

In Puglia, it's still common to see women out in the streets making orecchiette (little ears) pasta by hand. One of the most traditional preparations for orecchiette is with broccoli rabe. The bitter taste mellows as the broccoli rabe cooks, and the greens partially dissolve into a creamy sauce that coats the rough pasta brilliantly. Because orecchiette is a semolina pasta, you can either make it yourself (see How to Make Fresh Semolina Pasta on page 24) or use dry, store-bought pasta. The latter is perfectly fine, provided you look for a high-quality durum wheat pasta with a rough texture. Avoid anything that looks like smooth plastic discs.

DURATION: 30 minutes

YIELD: 3 or 4 servings

Salt

1 pound (450 g) broccoli rabe

¼ cup (60 ml) extra-virgin olive oil

2 cloves garlic, crushed with the skins on

5 anchovies (in oil)

2 teaspoons (10 g) tomato paste

12 ounces (340 g) dry orecchiette or 4 servings fresh orecchiette (page 24)

1. Bring a large pot of water to a rolling boil and salt it generously. Prep the broccoli rabe by removing and discarding any thick outer leaves and tougher stems, add it to the pot, and stir. Let the greens boil while you prepare the sauce.

2. In a large pan, heat the olive oil and garlic over medium heat. When the garlic starts to sizzle, reduce the heat to low and add the anchovies. Let them cook, stirring frequently, until they dissolve in the oil.

3. Use tongs or a slotted spoon to transfer the broccoli rabe to the pan and stir. Keep the broccoli rabe water simmering nearby. Add a ladleful of the water to the pan and bring to a simmer so that the greens can continue to cook.

4. Stir the tomato paste into the broccoli rabe, remove the garlic cloves, and salt the greens to taste. If you like, you can use some kitchen shears to cut the broccoli rabe up into smaller pieces as it cooks. (We like to do this; just be careful not to scratch your pan.)

5. Add the pasta to the boiling water (yes, the same water that the greens were cooked in) and cook it for 2 to 3 minutes less than the recommended al dente cook time on the package. If using fresh pasta, boil it for just 1 to 2 minutes. As the pasta cooks, you may need to add a little more water to the broccoli rabe to maintain moisture in the pan and keep the greens simmering.

6. Use a slotted spoon to transfer the cooked pasta to the pan. If necessary, spoon some more pasta water into the pan to keep the pasta cooking in liquid. Stir everything together over medium-high heat until the pasta is al dente to your taste. Stop adding water, allow the sauce to thicken, and serve immediately.

FRITTATA DI PASTA

⇥ *Pasta & Egg Omelet* ↤

Leftover pasta should never go to waste, but it also should never see the inside of a microwave. The best way to treat leftovers is to cook the pasta into an entirely new dish. A pasta frittata is a classic way to use up cold pasta the next day. If you try this dish, you'll soon be cooking extra spaghetti so that you have an excuse to make it. A pasta frittata works best with spaghetti, but other shapes can be used as well. If you end up with leftover pasta, try to keep it sauce-free, but toss it in olive oil before refrigerating. Doing this will prevent it from sticking together. The cheeses and meats are optional and very flexible. Feel free to substitute them with whatever you have on hand or prefer—this dish is a great fridge cleaner.

DURATION: 15 to 20 minutes

YIELD: 3 or 4 servings

---

3 to 5 large eggs (depending on the size of your pan)

About 3½ ounces (100 g) Parmigiano-Reggiano cheese, or to taste, grated

Salt and freshly ground black pepper

1 tablespoon (15 ml) extra-virgin olive oil

Chopped prosciutto cotto or ham (optional)

Cold cooked pasta (enough to fill a pan of your choice) or about 7 ounces (200 g) pasta (if cooking from scratch)

Chopped mozzarella cheese (optional)

1. In a large bowl, whisk the eggs with the Parmigiano cheese and a generous sprinkle of salt and pepper.

2. In a nonstick pan, heat the olive oil over medium heat. If adding meat, cook it in the oil for 1 to 2 minutes, stirring occasionally, to brown it slightly.

3. Add the cooked pasta and cook, stirring frequently for 2 to 3 minutes to soften it up, then spread it to evenly cover the bottom of the pan. Sprinkle the mozzarella on top (if using), then pour in the egg mixture. Use a spatula to evenly distribute the eggs among the pasta.

4. Cover the pan and let cook for about 2 minutes, or until the bottom of the frittata becomes lightly browned and crispy. Slide the frittata onto a flat plate or the pan lid. Place the pan on top of it and carefully flip the frittata so that the top can be cooked.

5. Return the pan to the stove and continue to cook, uncovered, until the new bottom is crispy.

6. Serve warm or at room temperature.

PASTA E PATATE

⤙ *Neapolitan Pasta with Potatoes* ⤚

This dish breaks about every pasta rule there is, but for good reason. While breaking pasta into pieces is normally a sin, this Neapolitan classic was formulated specifically to use the broken bits that are always present in the bottom of a pasta package. We recommend setting aside a big jar where you can collect these mixed bits of different pastas *(pasta mista)* until you have enough to make this dish. Casarecce is also a great shape for pasta e patate, plus you can even buy premade pasta mista from Italian importers. This dish is also unusual in that it's a true one-pot pasta, a rarity in Italy. The pasta isn't boiled; it's cooked directly in the sauce.

DURATION: 1 hour

YIELD: 3 or 4 servings

A leftover chunk of Parmigiano-Reggiano cheese rind (optional)

¼ cup (60 ml) extra-virgin olive oil

½ large white onion, diced

2 ribs celery, diced

1 large carrot, diced

2 ounces (55 g) pancetta or bacon, diced

2 large russet potatoes, peeled and cubed

Salt and freshly ground black pepper

15 cherry tomatoes, cut in half

10½ ounces (300 g) pasta mista or casarecce

Grated Parmigiano-Reggiano cheese (optional)

1. If using the Parmigiano rind, scrape the outer surface clean with a sharp knife and cut the rind into 1-inch (2.5 cm) chunks. Keep a kettle of warm water nearby.

2. In a medium saucepan, heat the olive oil over medium heat. Add the onion, celery, carrot, and pancetta and cook, stirring frequently, for 3 to 4 minutes, until the onion is tender and the pancetta has released its fat. Add the potatoes and cook for another 5 minutes, stirring frequently. Season with salt and pepper.

3. Add the tomatoes and the Parmigiano rind (if using) to the saucepan, then fill the pan with warm water until the potatoes are just barely submerged. Partially cover the pot, bring to a simmer, and let cook for 25 to 30 minutes, stirring occasionally.

4. Stir the pasta directly into the sauce and add more warm water until the pasta is submerged. Simmer for 10 to 12 minutes, until the pasta is al dente to your taste and the sauce is thick and creamy. If the water evaporates or is absorbed before the pasta is done, add a little more warm water to continue cooking.

5. Turn off the heat and stir in the Parmigiano, if using.

6. Serve hot or, perhaps even better, reheat it in a pan the next day. (And, yes, you can eat that deliciously gooey bite of Parmigiano rind.)

PENNE ALLA BOSCAIOLA

⇥ *Creamy Mushroom Pasta* ⇤

This meaty, creamy pasta comes from central Italy. There are many versions: some use guanciale or sausage instead of pancetta, some skip the tomato, and some don't have cream. We've chosen to include the latter to satisfy cream-lovers, who are often disappointed at how infrequently the ingredient is used in Italian cuisine. Boscaiola is a notable exception in a country that largely despises cream.

DURATION: 1 hour

YIELD: 3 or 4 servings

1½ ounces (40 g) dried mushrooms (see Note)

2 tablespoons (30 ml) extra-virgin olive oil

5½ ounces (155 g) pancetta, chopped

¼ large onion, diced

½ cup (120 ml) white wine

1 cup (240 ml) tomato (passata) puree

Salt and freshly ground black pepper

12 ounces (340 g) penne

¼ cup (60 ml) heavy cream

Grated Parmigiano-Reggiano, for topping

Chopped fresh parsley, for topping

1. Soak the dried mushrooms in a small bowl of warm water for 30 minutes. Remove the mushrooms, reserving the soaking water. Squeeze the excess liquid from them, then chop them. (The mushroom water will be used to add extra flavor to the pasta.)

2. In a large pan, heat the olive oil over medium heat. Add the pancetta and cook until it is lightly browned. With a slotted spoon, remove the pancetta and set it aside, leaving the oil and pancetta fat in the pan.

3. Add the onion to the pan and cook, stirring frequently, over medium heat until tender and slightly transparent. Add the mushrooms and cook for an additional 2 to 3 minutes. Add the wine, bring to a simmer, and let reduce until almost all the liquid has evaporated.

4. Add the tomato passata, ½ cup (120 ml) of the reserved mushroom soaking water (filter it through a fine-mesh sieve or cheesecloth), and a pinch each of salt and pepper. Bring to a gentle simmer and let cook for 15 minutes.

5. Meanwhile, bring a large pot of water to a boil and salt it generously. Add the penne and cook for 2 to 3 minutes less than the recommended al dente cook time on the package.

6. Stir the heavy cream into the sauce. Keep it on a very low simmer while the pasta finishes cooking.

7. Transfer the cooked pasta to the sauce with a slotted spoon. Stir everything together over medium heat until the pasta is al dente to your taste. The sauce should be thick and creamy, but feel free to add a little bit of pasta water if it thickens too much.

8. Serve immediately topped with plenty of grated Parmigiano and some chopped parsley.

NOTE *Try to find dried porcini mushrooms (fresh will also work, if you're lucky enough to have them). Other "gourmet" dried mushrooms will work fine in a pinch.*

PAPPARDELLE AI FUNGHI

⇥ *Fresh Pappardelle Pasta with Mushrooms* ↤

Eva's father, Papa Turi, is the best mushroom hunter in Dasà. During porcini season, he comes back from the mountain every day with huge baskets of mushrooms, which he then hoards in a chest freezer dedicated to the purpose. He won't even share his secret spots with us. This is his recipe for a classic pasta that varies widely throughout Italy.

DURATION: 30 minutes

YIELD: 3 or 4 servings

1 pound (450 g) fresh porcini mushrooms (see Note), chopped, or 4 ounces (115 g) dried mushrooms

¼ cup (60 ml) extra-virgin olive oil

2 tablespoons (30 g) unsalted butter

1 clove garlic, crushed with the skin on

15 to 20 cherry tomatoes, cut into quarters

1 whole fresh chili pepper (optional)

Salt and freshly ground black pepper

4 servings fresh pappardelle (see How to Make Fresh Egg Pasta on page 22)

Chopped fresh parsley, for topping

1. If using dried mushrooms, soak them in a bowl of warm water for 30 minutes. Drain, squeeze out the excess water, and chop them.

2. Put a large pot of water on to boil. While the water comes up to temperature, begin cooking the sauce.

3. In a large pan, heat the olive oil, butter, and garlic over medium heat. When the garlic starts to sizzle, add the mushrooms. Cook, stirring frequently, for 2 minutes, then add the tomatoes, chili pepper (if using), and a pinch each of salt and black pepper. Remove and discard the garlic clove. If using fresh mushrooms, they will naturally release quite a bit of water; if using dried mushrooms, spoon some pasta water into the pan and bring to a simmer. Let simmer for 4 to 5 minutes, then turn off the heat while you cook the pasta.

4. When the water comes to a rolling boil, salt it generously and add the fresh pasta. Stir once or twice to prevent sticking and boil for 2 to 3 minutes, until al dente to your taste.

5. Transfer the cooked pasta to the sauce with tongs. Stir everything together over medium heat until the sauce completely coats the pasta.

6. Serve immediately topped with chopped parsley.

NOTE *Fresh porcini mushrooms are definitely the way to go, if you can find them. If not, using about one-quarter of the amount (by weight) of dried mushrooms will work.*

TRENETTE AL PESTO

→| Pasta with Pesto, Potatoes & Green Beans |←

While there are many types of pesto in Italy, the most beloved is undoubtedly the basil-based pesto alla Genovese. In Genoa, one of the most classic pesto pasta dishes marries the sauce with linguine, potatoes, and green beans. The secret to making an excellent pesto is to avoid heating the delicate basil. Pesto should always be raw, as the basil completely changes its taste when cooked. For this reason, making the sauce in a stone mortar and pestle is by far the best option. Because a very large mortar and pestle isn't a terribly common kitchen tool, a blender or food processor can be used in a pinch. In this case, mix the ingredients in the same order, but do so by gently pulsing the machine. If you let the blender run full speed, the basil will overheat and become bitter.

DURATION: 1 hour

YIELD: 3 or 4 servings

6 cloves garlic, chopped

Coarse sea salt

2 tablespoons (20 g) pine nuts

2 ounces (60 g) fresh basil leaves

3 ounces (80 g) Parmigiano-Reggiano cheese, or to taste, grated

¼ cup (60 ml) extra-virgin olive oil

8 ounces (225 g) green beans, trimmed

1 large russet potato, peeled and cubed

12 ounces (340 g) linguine

1. Add the garlic and 2 generous pinches of sea salt to the bowl of a large stone mortar and pestle (you can make the pesto in batches if using a smaller mortar and pestle bowl). Using a circular grinding motion, mash the garlic into a paste. Add the pine nuts and grind them into a paste. Adding a small amount at a time, grind in the basil. When this is mashed into a paste (which can take some time, so be patient), grind in the Parmigiano. Finish by mixing in the olive oil. Taste the pesto and add more salt and/or cheese as desired.

2. Bring a large pot of water to a boil and salt it generously. Add the green beans and potatoes and boil them for 3 to 4 minutes. Add the linguine to the pot (yes, with the potatoes and green beans) and cook according to the package directions until al dente to your taste.

3. While the pasta boils, place the pesto into a large bowl and thin it with a few spoonfuls of pasta water; just enough to make a creamy sauce that can evenly coat the pasta.

4. Use tongs to transfer the cooked pasta and vegetables to the pesto bowl. Mix everything together until the sauce completely coats the pasta. If the sauce seems a little too thick, mix in a little more pasta water to thin it.

5. Serve immediately.

RAVIOLI RICOTTA E SPINACI

⊰ *Spinach & Ricotta Ravioli in Butter & Sage Sauce* ⊱

As long as Italians have been making stuffed pasta dumplings, they've been experimenting with all different manner of fillings. There are hundreds, if not thousands, of regional ravioli variations, but this Tuscan version has risen above the rest to be the "standard" recipe that everyone learns first. It's simple, delicious, and quite easy to make. In general, the philosophy behind ravioli maintains that the majority of the flavor is inside the pasta, so mild sauces are used to avoid covering up the existing taste. And a simple butter and sage sauce is the perfect choice. While you don't strictly need a pasta machine to make ravioli, it's a very useful tool in this case. It keeps the pasta sheets strictly uniform, so the dumplings cook evenly, and it naturally forms the dough into long strips that are perfect for assembly.

DURATION: 1 hour

YIELD: 12 to 15 ravioli; 4 servings

---

2 servings Fresh Egg Pasta dough (page 22)

1 tablespoon (15 ml) extra-virgin olive oil

3½ ounces (100 g) baby spinach

4½ ounces (130 g) ricotta, drained completely (see Note on page 106)

2 ounces (55 g) Parmigiano-Reggiano cheese, or to taste, grated

Pinch of grated nutmeg

Salt and freshly ground black pepper

All-purpose flour, for dusting

¼ cup (60 g) unsalted butter

8 to 10 fresh sage leaves

1. If it has not already rested, be sure to wrap the pasta dough in plastic and let sit for at least 30 minutes at room temperature. Prepare the filling while it rests.

2. In a large pan, heat the olive oil over medium heat. Add the spinach and cook, stirring occasionally, until the greens are completely wilted and tender, 5 to 8 minutes. Remove the spinach and finely chop it.

3. In a large bowl, stir together the chopped spinach, ricotta, and Parmigiano. Add the nutmeg and season with salt and pepper.

4. It is best to roll the pasta dough in batches. Cut the dough in half and keep the unused portion wrapped in plastic so that it does not dry out. Flatten the dough beneath your palm into a small pancake and lightly dust both sides with flour. Set your pasta machine rollers to the thickest setting (#0 on a standard Marcato Atlas 150 machine). Press one edge of the dough between the rollers while cranking the handle so that the pasta is pulled inward. Press the whole piece through and pull the resulting sheet of dough out from the bottom.

5. Adjust the rollers one setting narrower (e.g., from #0 to #1) and press the sheet through again. Repeat until you have rolled the pasta through the thinnest setting (#7, or 1.33 mm). If your pasta at any time sticks to the machine, lightly dust and rub it with flour. Cut the finished dough sheet in half, widthwise, so that you have two equal pieces of the same length.

continued on following page >>

6. Using two spoons, scoop up and place heaping teaspoons of spinach-ricotta filling down the middle of one pasta sheet, keeping each scoop about 1 inch (2.5 cm) from the pasta edges and 2 inches (5 cm) from each other. Drape the second sheet on top and carefully press it down around the stuffing to push excess air out. Use a ravioli cutter or knife to cut the pasta into squares, with about a ½-inch (13 mm) border around the stuffing. Press the edges firmly with your fingers so that they are completely sealed. Place the finished ravioli on a baking sheet or cutting board dusted with flour. Gather the dough scraps and repeat the rolling and shaping process until you have used all the pasta and/or stuffing, including the dough you set aside initially.

7. Bring a large pot of water to a boil and salt it generously. Add the butter and sage leaves to a large pan over low heat. Once the butter has melted completely, carefully drop the ravioli, one at a time, into the boiling water. Cook for 2 to 3 minutes, then transfer to the butter-sage sauce with a slotted spoon. Increase the heat to medium and gently toss the ravioli until completely coated in butter.

8. Serve immediately, topped with drizzled sauce and a few sage leaves from the pan.

NOTE *Ricotta sometimes needs to be drained in order to shed excess moisture. To do so, place it in a fine-mesh sieve suspended over a bowl. Cover with plastic wrap and let it drain overnight in the refrigerator.*

CICERI E TRIA

⤙ *Apulian-Style Pasta with Chickpeas* ⤚

In the past, it was quite common for pasta dough to be fried. This method has largely been lost in modern Italian cuisine, but ciceri e tria remains as a testament to this forgotten tradition. A portion of the homemade pasta is fried until crispy and then served atop the finished dish for extraordinary texture. What really makes this unusual dish stand out, though, is the incredible flavor of the simple sauce.

DURATION: 1½ hours, plus overnight soaking and drying

YIELD: 3 or 4 servings

---

7 ounces (200 g) dried chickpeas

1 teaspoon (5 g) baking soda

4 servings Fresh Semolina Pasta dough (page 24)

Semolina flour, for dusting

Salt

6 tablespoons (90 ml) extra-virgin olive oil, plus more for frying and drizzling

1 clove garlic, peeled

2 dried or fresh chili peppers, chopped

2 sprigs fresh rosemary

4 bay leaves

Pinch of freshly ground black pepper

1. Place the chickpeas in a bowl with the baking soda. Cover with water by 2 inches (5 cm). Let the chickpeas soak and the semolina dough dry overnight. Drain and rinse the chickpeas, reserving the cooking water. Place in a pot and cover with water. Bring to a boil and cook until soft but not mushy, about 1 hour, adding warm water as necessary to keep covered. Stir frequently by swirling the pot, never with a utensil. As they near completion, salt them. Turn off the heat.

2. Meanwhile, cut the dough in half. Keep one-half wrapped in plastic while you work on the other half. Roll out the dough with a rolling pin into a large circle about ¹⁄₁₆ inch (1.5 mm) thick. Dust the dough with flour as necessary to prevent sticking. Cut the circle in half, then slice each half into 1-inch-wide (2.5 cm) ribbons. Grasp each end of a ribbon strand with your fingers. Gently twist the ends in opposite directions until the ribbon forms a spiral tube. Place on a baking sheet. Twist the remaining ribbons, arranging them so they do not touch. Repeat with the remaining dough.

3. Fill a large pan with about 1 inch (2.5 cm) of oil and heat to frying temperature (see How to Fry at Home on page 34). Working in batches, fry one-third of the dry pasta until golden brown (it cooks fast). Remove with a slotted spoon to a paper towel–lined plate to drain. Sprinkle with salt.

4. Bring a large pot of water to a boil and salt it generously. Meanwhile, heat the 6 tablespoons (90 ml) oil and garlic in a large pan over medium heat. When the garlic starts to sizzle, add the chili peppers, rosemary, and bay leaves. Use a slotted spoon to transfer the chickpeas to the pan and spoon in just enough of the reserved cooking water to get a simmer going while you cook the pasta, adding more chickpea water as necessary. When the water comes to a rolling boil, add the pasta and cook until al dente to your taste. Transfer the cooked pasta to the pan with a slotted spoon and add the black pepper. Stir everything together over medium-high heat until the pasta is evenly coated.

5. Serve immediately topped with a drizzle of olive oil and the fried pasta.

PASTA ALLA NORMA

⊰ *Fried Eggplant & Tomato Pasta* ⊱

This pasta is named after the opera *Norma,* because the dish is considered to be as sublime as Bellini's music. While we hesitate to give it such a strong title as Our Favorite Pasta, it's worth noting that in private conversation we use pasta alla Norma as the yardstick against which we measure all other dishes: "It's really good, but would I eat it instead of a Norma?" In short, it's a dish that we believe everyone should try at some point in their life.

DURATION: 45 minutes

YIELD: 3 or 4 servings

Extra-virgin olive oil, for frying (this is a must; there are no substitutions when it comes to frying eggplants)

2 large eggplants, cut into 1-inch (2.5 cm) cubes (optionally, save a few thin, round slices of eggplant for topping)

Salt

12 ounces (340 g) rigatoni

2 cups (480 ml) Simple Tomato Sauce (page 32)

4 or 5 fresh basil leaves, torn into small pieces

Grated ricotta salata cheese (see Note), for topping

1. Fill a large, deep frying pan with about 3 inches (7.5 cm) of olive oil and bring up to frying temperature (see How to Fry at Home on page 34). Working in batches if necessary, carefully drop in the eggplant cubes and fry them, stirring gently, until lightly browned on all sides, 2 to 3 minutes. Remove with a slotted spoon to a bowl. (It's important not to drain the fried eggplant on a paper towel, as you need that flavored oil in the sauce.) If you saved a few eggplant slices for topping, fry those now until browned on all sides and transfer to a paper towel–lined plate to drain. Save the frying oil for drizzling later.

2. Bring a large pot of water to a boil and salt it generously. Add the rigatoni and cook for 2 to 3 minutes less than the recommended al dente cook time on the package.

3. Add the fried eggplant (plus any oil that drained into the bowl) and the simple tomato sauce to a clean, large pan. Bring the sauce to a gentle simmer and stir everything together well. If the sauce thickens too much while the pasta cooks, thin it with a little pasta water.

4. Use a slotted spoon to transfer the cooked pasta to the sauce. Stir everything together over medium-high heat for about 2 minutes, or until the pasta is al dente to your taste. Stir in the basil.

5. Serve immediately topped with the fried eggplant slices (if using), a drizzle of the frying oil, and plenty of grated ricotta salata.

NOTE *If you can't find ricotta salata, you can substitute it with pecorino or Parmigiano-Reggiano.*

GNOCCHI ALLA SORRENTINA

⊰ Baked Gnocchi, Tomato Sauce & Mozzarella ⊱

Travelers often ask us what they should eat while visiting the Amalfi Coast. Our first answer is always gnocchi alla Sorrentina. The dish can seem a little strange: you might find yourself wondering why you went through all the trouble of making these delicate pillows of potato pasta just to bake them all together. Once you taste it, you'll understand. When well made, the gnocchi bake beautifully into a dish in which each piece blends with the next yet retains its individual form and texture.

DURATION: 30 minutes

YIELD: 6 servings

---

6 cups (1.5 L) Simple Tomato Sauce (page 32)

Salt

6 or 7 servings Fresh Potato Gnocchi (page 30)

4 ounces (110 g) mozzarella cheese, chopped, divided

3½ ounces (100 g) Parmigiano-Reggiano cheese, or to taste, grated, divided

1. Preheat the oven to 415°F (215°C). Warm the simple tomato sauce in a saucepan and preheat an oven to 415°F (215°C).

2. Bring a large pot of water to a boil and salt it generously. Cook the gnocchi as directed in step 6 on page 31.

3. Meanwhile, spread a layer of simple tomato sauce in the bottom of a 2-quart (2 L) baking dish and add 1 to 2 ladlefuls of the sauce to a large bowl.

4. When the gnocchi are cooked, use a slotted spoon to transfer them to the bowl. Ladle most of the remaining tomato sauce into the bowl, reserving some for topping. Using a silicone spatula, gently mix the gnocchi and tomato sauce together.

5. Ladle half of the gnocchi into the baking dish and spread it out evenly. Top this with half of the chopped mozzarella and half of the grated Parmigiano, then add the remaining gnocchi to the dish and spread it evenly. Top the entire dish with the remaining mozzarella and tomato sauce. Evenly sprinkle the rest of the Parmigiano all over.

6. Bake for 10 to 15 minutes, until the cheese melts and the top becomes slightly crispy. Let cool for 10 minutes before serving.

CANNELLONI

⤙ *Baked Stuffed Pasta Rolls* ⤚

Cannelloni, commonly called "manicotti" in the United States, are stuffed rolls of fresh pasta, baked together like a lasagna (see Lasagna alla Bolognese on page 120) or Pasta al Forno (page 114). It's a classic Sunday lunch dish for a big group of people, and it is also great to keep in the freezer for an excellent meal when there's little time to cook. Freeze it fully cooked, then simply thaw and reheat it in a warm oven. While it's possible to roll cannelloni by hand, we highly recommend using a pasta machine.

DURATION: 1½ hours

YIELD: 6 servings

1 tablespoon (15 ml) extra-virgin olive oil

10 ounces (285 g) baby spinach

17½ ounces (500 g) ricotta

1 large egg

5½ ounces (155 g) Parmigiano-Reggiano cheese, grated, plus more for topping

Pinch of ground nutmeg

Salt and freshly ground black pepper

3 servings Fresh Egg Pasta dough (page 22)

All-purpose flour, for dusting

2¼ cups (540 ml) Simple Tomato Sauce (page 32)

2⅛ cups (500 ml) Besciamella (halve the recipe on page 33)

1. In a large pan, heat the olive oil over medium heat. Add the spinach and cook, stirring occasionally, until it is completely tender and wilted, 5 minutes. Let the spinach cool to the touch, squeeze out the excess liquid, and finely chop it.

2. In a large bowl, combine the chopped spinach, ricotta, egg, Parmigiano, nutmeg, and a generous sprinkle each of salt and black pepper and mix well. Chill the mixture in the refrigerator while you roll out the pasta.

3. Bring a large pot of water to a boil. Cut off about one-third of the pasta dough, keeping the rest wrapped in plastic. Flatten the dough beneath your palm into a small pancake and lightly dust both sides with flour. Set your pasta machine rollers to the thickest setting (#0 on a standard Marcato Atlas 150 machine). Press one edge of the dough between the rollers while cranking the handle so that the pasta is pulled inward. Press the whole piece through and pull the resulting sheet of dough out from the bottom. Adjust the rollers one setting narrower (e.g., from #0 to #1) and press the sheet through again. Repeat until you have rolled the pasta through the thinnest setting (#7, or 1.33 mm). If your pasta sticks to the machine, lightly dust and rub it with flour.

4. Cut the dough sheet into 4½-inch (11.5 cm) squares. (We cook the cannelloni in a 9 × 13-inch, or 23 × 33-cm, lasagna dish, which means the pasta rolls can fit in side by side, but if you use a different-size pan, you can adjust the length of one side of the squares to half the width of your pan.) Arrange the cut pieces on a clean towel so that they do not overlap. Gather the remaining scraps, add them to another one-third of the dough, roll it out, and cut into squares. Repeat with the remaining dough, until all of it is cut into squares. You should end up with 18 to 20 squares.

5. Salt the boiling water generously. Working with 2 or 3 pasta squares at a time, carefully drop them into the water and boil until they float to the top, 20 to 30 seconds. Remove with tongs and lay them back on the towel so that they do not touch each other.

6. Preheat the oven to 400°F (205°C).

7. Spread a thin layer of the simple tomato sauce to cover the bottom of a 9 × 13-inch (23 × 33 cm) lasagna baking dish. Spoon 1½ to 2 tablespoons (25 to 30 g) of the spinach-ricotta filling along one edge of a cooked pasta square in an even line, about 1 inch (2.5 cm) wide and tall. Gently roll up the pasta square to cover the stuffing, then place the roll in the lasagna pan. The rolls should be arranged such that two can fit end to end along the width of the pan. Continue to fill the remaining cooked pasta squares and place in the bottom of the pan in a single layer of rolls.

8. Spread the remaining tomato sauce over the rolls in an even layer, followed by the besciamella spread evenly on top of the tomato sauce. Top the cannelloni with a generous grating of Parmigiano.

9. Cover the dish with foil and bake for 20 minutes. Remove the foil and bake for an additional 20 minutes. Let cool for 10 minutes before serving.

PASTA AL FORNO

⇥ *Baked Pasta* ⇤

Pasta al forno literally means "baked pasta." There is no one way to make a pasta al forno; in fact, it's a great fridge cleaner, in which you can use whatever cold cuts, cheese, or cooked meat you happen to have. Usually, baked pasta dishes are either red (with tomato sauce, page 32) or white (with besciamella, page 33). As long as you follow the basic principle of undercooking the pasta (rigatoni or other short tubes are recommended) and giving the dish enough sauce so it stays moist, you can get very creative. This Calabrian-style recipe includes some typical and classic ingredients: hard-boiled eggs, fried meatballs, and chopped mozzarella cheese. Feel free to substitute salami, ham, or cooked sausage for the meatballs. The mozzarella can be replaced by any type of cheese that melts well when baked.

DURATION: 2½ hours

YIELD: 4 to 6 servings

½ pound (225 g) ground beef, pork, or veal, or any combo of the three

3½ ounces (100 g) pecorino cheese, grated, divided

3½ ounces (100 g) Parmigiano-Reggiano cheese, grated, divided

1 large egg

2 tablespoons (7 g) chopped fresh parsley

Salt and freshly ground black pepper

About ½ cup (45 g) fresh bread crumbs, or to taste

Extra-virgin olive oil (or other neutral oil), for frying

12 ounces (340 g) rigatoni

6 cups (1.4 L) Simple Tomato Sauce (double the recipe on page 32)

3 hard-boiled eggs, chopped

3½ ounces (100 g) mozzarella cheese, chopped

1. Combine the ground meat with half of the pecorino and half of the Parmigiano, the egg, the parsley, several generous pinches of salt, and a generous sprinkle of pepper. Begin to mix the ingredients together by hand, while gradually adding enough bread crumbs until the mixture is slightly tacky but not wet or sticky. Roll the meat mixture into 1-inch (2.5 cm) balls.

2. Fill a large, deep pan with 2 inches (5 cm) of oil and heat to frying temperature (see How to Fry at Home on page 34). Working in batches, fry the meatballs until they are browned on all sides. Use a slotted spoon to remove the meatballs to a paper towel–lined plate to drain. When the meatballs have cooled to the touch, cut them in half.

3. Preheat the oven to 400°F (205°C). Bring a large pot of water to a boil and salt it generously. Boil the pasta as directed on the package, but only cook it for half of the recommended al dente cook time. Drain the pasta using a colander and return it to the pot.

4. Add the simple tomato sauce to the cooked pasta and mix thoroughly. Add the meatballs, chopped eggs, chopped mozzarella, and half of the remaining grated cheeses. Spread the pasta mix evenly into a 2-quart (2 L) baking dish and evenly top it with the remaining grated cheese.

5. Cover the dish with aluminum foil and bake for 30 minutes. Remove the foil and bake for an additional 10 minutes, or until the top begins to crisp. Let cool for 10 minutes before serving. The fully cooked pasta al forno (or any leftovers) can be frozen for later and reheated in a warm oven after thawing.

PASTA ALLA CARBONARA

→ Egg, Cheese & Guanciale Pasta ←

The famous Roman pasta alla carbonara is made with guanciale, eggs, pecorino, and black pepper. Full stop. The addition of peas, parsley, cream, mushrooms, and so on might make a good pasta, but it won't be a real carbonara. With a dish this simple, even the tiniest change in ingredients makes an enormous impact, so Romans are hardly overreacting when they protest strange additions. The one generally accepted substitution is the use of pancetta or bacon instead of guanciale, but only in cases in which the latter is impossible to find. These days, guanciale is widely available online and in Italian markets. It has a wonderful and unique taste, so we highly recommend seeking out the real deal. Romans debate among themselves about which pasta shape works best in a carbonara. Some insist on a long pasta (such as spaghetti) while others maintain that a short pasta (such as rigatoni) is superior. We love both, so we'll leave the argument to the Romans and keep enjoying this incredible classic with whichever we have on hand.

DURATION: 20 minutes

YIELD: 3 or 4 servings

Salt

12 ounces (340 g) rigatoni or spaghetti

4½ ounces (125 g) guanciale, outer skin trimmed and cut into ½-inch (13 mm) cubes (or substitute pancetta cut into ½-inch, or 13-mm, cubes)

4 large eggs

2 ounces (55 g) pecorino cheese, grated. plus more for topping

Freshly ground black pepper

1. Bring a large pot of water to a rolling boil and salt it lightly (the guanciale and pecorino are quite salty, so in this case, use about half the salt you would normally add). Add the pasta and cook as directed on the package until al dente to your taste.

2. Meanwhile, place the guanciale in a large pan over medium heat. (If using pancetta, lightly season it with a pinch each of salt and pepper.) Cook, stirring occasionally, for 4 to 6 minutes, until deeply browned and crispy. Turn off the heat.

3. Separate the eggs, placing the yolks in a large bowl. If you prefer a slightly thinner sauce, add 1 egg white; otherwise, save the egg whites for another use. Add the pecorino and a generous sprinkle of black pepper, then whisk together the eggs and cheese until thoroughly mixed.

4. Transfer the hot, cooked pasta to the egg mixture using tongs or a slotted spoon. Stir vigorously until the sauce completely coats the pasta, then add the guanciale and the fat from the pan into the bowl (see Note). Stir again to evenly mix the sauce. Serve immediately topped with more black pepper.

NOTE *Yes, the eggs are mixed into the pasta raw. Cooking them together in a pan risks resulting in stringy scrambled eggs rather than a velvety sauce. Old Italian wisdom maintains that the hot pasta pasteurizes the eggs and renders them safe to eat. If you're still nervous, vigorously mix the pasta and sauce in a heat-resistant bowl that can be placed over the simmering pasta water, a bain-marie. This is a gentler way to cook the eggs.*

MINESTRONE

⇥ *Vegetable Soup with Ditalini Pasta* ⇤

Minestrone is the most common soup eaten throughout Italy. There's no one way to make it, so feel free to adapt it with vegetables you have on hand or that are in season. What's important is that the ingredients are added in stages, with those taking longest to cook being added first and those with shorter cook times later.

DURATION: 1½ hours, plus overnight soaking

YIELD: 4 to 6 servings

---

1 cup (140 g) dried borlotti beans

2 or 3 sprigs fresh rosemary and thyme

¼ cup (60 ml) extra-virgin olive oil

½ large onion, diced

3 tablespoons (45 ml) tomato passata (puree)

1 medium russet potato, peeled and cubed

1 rib celery, chopped

½ large carrot, peeled and chopped

7 ounces (200 g) butternut squash, peeled and cubed

1 large leek, thinly sliced

½ large head cauliflower, broken into bite-size florets

4 ounces (120 g) kale, chopped

1 large zucchini, chopped

5 stalks asparagus, chopped

A piece of Parmigiano-Reggiano rind (optional)

¼ cup (40 g) frozen peas

Salt

4½ ounces (125 g) ditalini (see Note)

3 or 4 fresh basil leaves, torn (or a few spoonfuls of pesto alla Genovese on page 102)

1. Soak the borlotti beans overnight, then drain completely.

2. Tie the herb sprigs into a bundle with butcher's twine.

3. In a large pot, heat the olive oil over medium-high heat. Add the onion and cook, stirring frequently, until tender and slightly transparent, 2 to 3 minutes.

4. Except where noted, the procedure for gradually adding the vegetables is the same for each ingredient and can be repeated. Add the beans, herb bundle, and tomato passata and stir them into the onions. Add warm water until the beans are covered. Bring the soup to a simmer and let cook for about 5 minutes before adding the next ingredient and repeating the process. Do so with the potato, celery, and carrot (added together); the squash, leek, cauliflower, and kale (added individually); and the zucchini and asparagus (added together). Each time you add a vegetable(s), add more warm water as necessary to keep the ingredients covered, then bring the soup back to a simmer for 5 minutes.

5. After adding the zucchini and asparagus, add 1½ cups (360 ml) warm water so that there is some excess liquid that can evaporate. Partially cover the pot and let simmer for 15 to 20 minutes.

6. If using the Parmigiano rind, scrape the outer surface clean with a sharp knife. Add the frozen peas and cheese rind (if using). Salt the soup to taste, partially cover the pot again, and let simmer for an additional 10 minutes. If the soup thickens too much for your liking, add more warm water.

7. Add the ditalini and basil (if using pesto, stir it in right before serving). Let simmer, uncovered, for the recommended cook time on the pasta package, or until the pasta is al dente to your taste.

8. Serve hot.

NOTE *A minestrone is usually thickened with a grain, often ditalini pasta (tiny tubes). Feel free to substitute it with broken spaghetti pieces or pasta mista, arborio rice, barley, or spelt.*

SPAGHETTI ALLE VONGOLE

↦ *Spaghetti with Clams* ↤

Spaghetti with clams is a classic, simple seafood pasta. Like all simple recipes, it depends upon using the right ingredients. Avoid large clams, which will be very tough and chewy, and search out some very small varieties, such as littleneck or Manila clams. Once the sauce is cooked you can either leave the clams in their shells or remove and discard the shells. In the latter case, we recommend leaving at least a third of the clams in their shells for aesthetic purposes.

DURATION: 20 minutes, plus
3 hours soaking

YIELD: 3 or 4 servings

2 pounds (900 g) littleneck or Manila clams

Salt

5 tablespoons (75 ml) extra-virgin olive oil

1 clove garlic, peeled

1 cup (240 ml) white wine

Freshly ground black pepper

12 ounces (340 g) spaghetti

Chopped fresh parsley, for topping

1. Prep the clams to remove sand and sediment: Fill a large bowl with water and stir in enough salt so that it tastes like seawater. Soak the clams in the salt water for 3 hours, then drain and rinse them.

2. Put a large pot of water on to boil. While the water comes up to temperature, begin cooking the sauce.

3. In a large pan, heat the olive oil and garlic over medium heat. When the garlic starts to sizzle, add the clams, increase the heat to high, and cover the pan. Let the clams cook until the shells open, about 5 minutes. Add the wine, reduce the heat to medium-low, and bring it to a gentle simmer. After a few minutes, when the smell of alcohol has dissipated, season the sauce with a pinch of black pepper. (Don't salt the sauce, as the clams should be plenty salty.) Turn off the heat and let the sauce rest while the pasta cooks.

4. When the water comes to a rolling boil, salt it generously and add the spaghetti. Cook it for 2 to 3 minutes less than the recommended al dente cook time on the package.

5. Using tongs or a spaghetti fork, transfer the cooked pasta to the sauce and add a few spoonfuls of pasta water to the pan. Stir the pasta and sauce together over medium heat until the pasta is al dente to your taste. If the sauce thickens too much and the pasta needs more time to cook, add a little more pasta water.

6. Serve immediately with plenty of clams on the plate and topped with chopped parsley.

LASAGNA ALLA BOLOGNESE

⇥ Bologna-Style Lasagna ⇤

While there are many lasagna variations in Italy, this is *the* lasagna. It takes patience to make, because using fresh egg pasta and homemade ragù is an absolute must. If you put in the effort, you and your guests will be rewarded with a lasagna beyond all expectation. This is the kind of dish where one bite will ruin all other lasagne for you. You've been warned. To make things a little easier, you can make the ragù and pasta dough a day or two in advance. This is one of the few cases when we recommend using a pasta machine, as it will help manage the large amount needed and result in very even layers. That being said, you don't absolutely need one—we often turn to a rolling pin.

DURATION: 3 to 5 hours; up to 8 hours if making the ragù and pasta dough the same day

YIELD: 4 to 6 servings

Salt

3½ ounces (100 g) baby spinach

3⅓ cups (400 g) all-purpose flour, plus more for dusting

3 large eggs

5 cups (1.2 L) Ragù alla Bolognese (page 78)

3 cups (700 ml) Besciamella (page 33)

9 ounces (250 g) mozzarella cheese, or to taste, chopped

3 ounces (85 g) Parmigiano-Reggiano cheese, or to taste, grated

1. Bring a large pot of water to a boil and salt it generously. Add the baby spinach and boil for 1 to 2 minutes, until it is wilted and very tender. Drain with a slotted spoon, reserving the cooking water, and let the spinach cool to the touch. Squeeze out the excess water and mince the cooked spinach.

2. Pour the flour into a pile on a large, clean work surface and hollow out the center with your hand so that it looks like a volcano. Crack the eggs into the center, then add the minced spinach.

3. Whisk the eggs and spinach with a fork while gradually incorporating some of the surrounding flour. Once a thick paste has formed, fold in the remaining flour and begin kneading by hand. Knead the dough until it is consistent and uniform, about 10 minutes; it should be soft but not sticky. (Don't worry if the dough does not absorb all the flour; pasta is smart stuff and will take what it needs. On the other hand, if the dough is sticky, dust it with more flour.)

4. Form the pasta dough into a ball, wrap it in plastic, and let rest at room temperature for 30 minutes, or refrigerate overnight if making it in advance.

5. Now it is time to roll out the pasta dough into lasagna sheets. If using a pasta machine, cut off about one-quarter of the dough with a knife and keep the remainder wrapped in plastic so that it does not dry out. Start rolling with the thickest setting (usually #1) and gradually increase the number until you reach the correct thinness: Dust the dough lightly with flour before rolling and each time it comes out of the machine. Roll out the dough into a long sheet (feel free to cut it in half at any point if it gets too long to manage) until it is about $1/16$ inch (2 mm) thick (the #5 setting on a standard Marcato Atlas machine). If using a rolling pin, cut off about one-third of the dough and keep the remainder wrapped. Roll it out into a big circle on a large, smooth work surface and dust the dough liberally with flour as you work. Flip it over often as you roll it out. When the dough is about $1/16$ inch (2 mm) thick, it is ready to cut.

6. Cut the pasta sheets into large rectangles, about 8 × 5 inches (20 × 13 cm), but do not worry about being precise. (The pasta will inevitably and unavoidably be trimmed and layered in a sort of patchwork, so don't worry about making perfect squares. Rounded corners aren't a big deal either.) Hang on to little scraps or smaller pieces as those can be useful later.

7. Lay the cut pasta sheets flat on clean kitchen towels without overlapping them. Repeat the rolling and cutting process until all the remaining pasta dough is finished. While you work, bring the pot of spinach water back up to a rolling boil.

8. Working in batches of 2 or 3 lasagna sheets at a time, drop the sheets into the boiling water and cook for about 30 seconds each. Gently remove each sheet with tongs and lay it back on the same towel. (It is especially important to ensure the pasta sheets don't touch each other at this point; they will stick together like glue.) Repeat until all the pasta is cooked.

continued on following page >>

9. Preheat the oven to 400°F (205°C).

10. Spread a thin layer of ragù in the bottom of a 2-quart (2 L) baking dish. Drizzle a few spoonfuls of besciamella on top and spread it into the ragù. Assemble a single layer of pasta sheets on top (the individual pieces can overlap slightly). Cut pasta pieces to fit so that you can fill any holes and corners that might be exposed. On top of the pasta, spread a generous layer of ragù, followed by an even spread of some chopped mozzarella, a drizzle of besciamella, and a dusting of grated Parmigiano. Now, repeat the layers—pasta, ragù, mozzarella, besciamella, Parmigiano—until you have filled the dish; you should end up with 4 or 5 layers in all.

11. Finish with a final layer of pasta. Over the pasta, spread a thick layer of ragù and besciamella. Mix them together and make sure they completely cover the pasta from corner to corner. Top it all off with a generous grating of Parmigiano. Cover the lasagna loosely with aluminum foil.

12. Bake for 30 minutes, then remove the foil and bake for an additional 20 to 25 minutes, until the cheese on top is slightly crispy. Let cool for 20 minutes before serving.

RISO

⊰ Rice ⊱

After pasta, rice is one of the more common options for a first course. Italian rice dishes tend to embrace—nay, amplify—the natural starchiness of the native grain varieties, of which there are over two hundred. It's an oft-overlooked staple of Italian cuisine that deserves to be held in the same international regard as pasta. If you have never cooked a risotto before, consider trying Risotto al Parmigiano (page 130) first to master the basic technique.

INSALATA DI RISO

⊰| *Cold Rice Salad* |⊱

The appeal of cold pasta salads is understandable, but we (along with many Italians) think there's a better option: rice salads. When left cold, even the most al dente pasta becomes soft and mushy. Rice, on the other hand, holds its texture very well. This is a classic picnic dish in Italy. Visit the beach during summer and you're sure to see a bowl of insalata di riso being passed around. There are many ways to make a rice salad, but we've chosen a mix of ingredients that create perfect, tangy freshness for a hot summer day. You'll need a jar of giardiniera, a mix of pickled vegetables that is available in most grocery stores (check the olive section).

DURATION: 45 minutes, plus
3 hours chilling (best made a day in advance)

YIELD: 6 servings

Salt

1½ cups (375 g) carnaroli, arborio, or vialone nano rice

1 jar (16 ounces, or 454 g) giardiniera vegetable mix, drained

6 ounces (170 g) prosciutto cotto or ham, cubed

6 ounces (170 g) provolone or Swiss cheese, cubed

5 ounces, or 150 g, whole-chunk tuna in olive oil, drained

2 hard-boiled eggs, chopped

About 20 pitted Kalamata olives

Juice from 2 to 3 lemons

¼ cup (60 ml) extra-virgin olive oil

1. Bring a large pot of water to a boil and salt it generously. Add the rice and cook as directed on the package. (The recommended al dente cook time is probably a safe bet, but it's important not to overcook the rice, so we advise cooking it to taste and erring on the side of being undercooked.)

2. While the rice cooks, mix the giardiniera, prosciutto cotto, cheese, tuna, eggs, and olives in a large bowl.

3. Drain the cooked rice and add it to the bowl along with the lemon juice and olive oil. Stir everything together. (You shouldn't need more salt if the rice was properly seasoned, but feel free to salt to taste if necessary.)

4. Let the salad cool to room temperature before covering and chilling in the refrigerator for at least 3 hours.

5. Serve cold. It is best the next day and will last for 4 to 5 days stored in an airtight container in the refrigerator.

RISOTTO ALLA MILANESE

❧ *Saffron Risotto* ❧

In order to technically be considered "alla Milanese," this saffron risotto should be served with Ossobuco alla Milanese (page 147), one of the rare cases when first and second courses are plated together. You can certainly skip the meat, in which case the dish becomes risotto allo Zafferano. In any case, it's one of the most beloved risotti for good reason.

DURATION: 30 minutes

YIELD: 3 or 4 servings

---

8 cups (2 L) beef stock (substitute chicken or vegetable broth for a lighter color)

Salt

1⅓ cups (320 g) carnaroli, arborio, or vialone nano rice

½ cup (120 g) unsalted butter, divided

2 tablespoons (30 g) beef bone marrow (optional; see Note)

½ large white onion, diced

¾ cup (175 ml) white wine

1 teaspoon (1 g) saffron

3½ ounces (100 g) Parmigiano-Reggiano cheese, grated

1. In a medium pot, warm the stock on the stovetop; it does not need to boil or simmer. The saltiness of the stock is what will season the risotto. Most store-bought broths are already plenty salty, but if using a homemade broth, be sure to salt it to taste.

2. Meanwhile, add the rice to a small skillet and toast over medium heat for 2 to 3 minutes, stirring or tossing frequently to avoid burning it. Remove from the heat.

3. Add ¼ cup (60 g) of the butter, the bone marrow (if using), and the onion to a large pan or shallow pot (a sauté pan works well). Cook, stirring frequently, over medium heat until the onion is tender and slightly translucent, 2 to 3 minutes. Add the rice and stir everything together until the rice is completely coated in butter.

4. Pour in the wine, reduce the heat to medium-low, and bring to a simmer. Let simmer until the rice has absorbed almost all the liquid. Use a ladle to spoon in just enough of the warm stock to submerge the rice, then bring to a gentle simmer. Continue to simmer the rice, stirring occasionally and adding a little more broth as needed, to maintain the liquid in the pan, until the rice is fully cooked; it usually takes 15 to 17 minutes for the rice to reach al dente but consult the recommended cook time on the package and trust your taste.

5. While the risotto cooks, mix the saffron into ¼ cup (60 ml) of the warm stock, then pour into the risotto. When the rice is about 2 minutes from reaching al dente, stop adding stock so that the risotto thickens slightly. When the rice is cooked to your taste and the consistency of the risotto is creamy but not soupy, turn off the heat. Stir in the remaining ¼ cup (60 g) butter and the Parmigiano. Cover the pan and let the risotto rest for 2 to 3 minutes before serving.

NOTE *If you can't find beef bone marrow, ask your local butcher. They often sell raw marrow bones for pets, but they're perfectly fine for human consumption.*

RISOTTO AL PARMIGIANO

⤜ *Cheese Risotto* ⤛

This is probably the simplest risotto there is, which is why it's the perfect recipe for those who are just learning how to cook Italian rice. The ingredients and techniques used to make risotto al Parmigiano are present in almost every other risotto recipe, so mastering this simple dish opens up a lot of doors for variations. That being said, don't be tempted to think that this is a mere training dish. Cheese lovers will adore it, and skeptics will be forced to admit that, sometimes, simpler is better.

DURATION: 30 minutes

YIELD: 3 or 4 servings

8 cups (2 L) vegetable broth

Salt

1⅓ cups (320 g) carnaroli, arborio, or vialone nano rice

3 tablespoons (45 g) unsalted butter, divided

½ large white onion, diced

¾ cup (175 ml) white wine

3½ ounces (100 g) Parmigiano-Reggiano cheese, grated

1. In a medium pot, warm the broth on the stovetop; it does not need to boil or simmer. The saltiness of the stock is what will season the risotto. Most store-bought broths are already plenty salty, but if using a homemade broth, be sure to salt it to taste.

2. Meanwhile, add the rice to a small skillet and toast over medium-high heat for 2 to 3 minutes, stirring or tossing frequently to avoid burning it. Remove from the heat.

3. In a large pan or shallow pot (a sauté pan works well), add 2 tablespoons (30 g) of the butter and the onion. Cook, stirring frequently, over medium heat until the onion is tender and slightly translucent, 2 to 3 minutes. Add the rice and stir everything together until the rice is completely coated in butter.

4. Pour in the wine, reduce the heat to medium-low, and bring to a simmer. Let simmer until the rice has absorbed almost all the liquid. Use a ladle to spoon in just enough of the warm broth to submerge the rice, then bring the risotto to a gentle simmer. Continue to simmer the rice, stirring occasionally and adding a little more broth as needed to maintain the liquid in the pan, until the rice is fully cooked; it usually takes 15 to 17 minutes for the rice to reach al dente but consult the recommended cook time on the package and trust your taste. When the rice is about 2 minutes away from reaching al dente, stop adding broth so that the risotto thickens slightly.

5. When the rice is cooked to your taste and the consistency of the risotto is creamy but not soupy, turn off the heat. Stir in the remaining 1 tablespoon (15 g) butter and the Parmigiano. Cover the pan and let the risotto rest for 2 to 3 minutes before serving.

RISOTTO AI FUNGHI

⤚ *Mushroom Risotto* ⤙

In Italy, mushroom risotto is normally made with fresh porcini mushrooms. The difficulty of finding this ingredient has led us to slightly adapt tradition with a recipe that works with dried mushrooms.

DURATION: 1 hour

YIELD: 3 or 4 servings

1½ ounces (40 g) dried porcini mushrooms (or other dried "gourmet" mushrooms)

8 cups (2 L) vegetable broth

Salt (optional)

1⅓ cups (320 g) carnaroli, arborio, or vialone nano rice

3 tablespoons (45 g) unsalted butter, divided

½ large onion, diced

¾ cup (175 ml) white wine

Pinch of freshly ground black pepper

3½ ounces (100 g) Parmigiano-Reggiano cheese, grated

1. Soak the dried mushrooms in a bowl of warm water for 30 minutes. Remove the mushrooms, reserving the soaking water. Squeeze the excess liquid from the mushrooms, then chop them.

2. In a medium pot, warm the broth on the stovetop; it does not need to boil or simmer. The saltiness of the broth is what will season the risotto. Most store-bought broths are already plenty salty, but if using a homemade broth, be sure to salt it to taste.

3. Meanwhile, add the rice to a small skillet and toast it over medium heat for 2 to 3 minutes, stirring or tossing frequently to avoid burning it. Remove from the heat.

4. Add 2 tablespoons (30 g) of the butter and the onion to a large pan or shallow pot (a sauté pan works well). Cook, stirring frequently, over medium heat until the onion is tender and slightly transparent, 2 to 3 minutes. Add the mushrooms and cook for 2 to 3 minutes. Add the rice and stir everything together until the rice is completely coated in butter.

5. Pour in the wine, reduce the heat to medium-low, and bring to simmer. Let simmer until the rice has absorbed almost all the liquid. Strain the reserved mushroom soaking water through a fine-mesh sieve and add it to the rice. Use a ladle to spoon in just enough of the warm broth to submerge the rice, then bring the risotto to a gentle simmer. Continue to simmer the rice, stirring occasionally and adding a little more broth as needed, to maintain the liquid in the pan, until the rice is fully cooked; it usually takes 15 to 17 minutes for the rice to reach al dente but consult the recommended cook time on the package and trust your taste. When the rice is about 2 minutes away from reaching al dente, add the pepper and stop adding broth so that the risotto thickens slightly.

6. When the rice is cooked to your taste and the consistency of the risotto is creamy but not soupy, turn off the heat and stir in the remaining 1 tablespoon (15 g) butter and the Parmigiano. Cover the pot and let the risotto rest for 2 to 3 minutes before serving.

RISOTTO AL POMODORO

⇥ *Tomato Risotto* ⇤

This is perhaps our favorite risotto of all time. Maybe we're biased due to a tomato sauce addiction, but we stand by our assertion that everyone should try risotto al pomodoro at least once. It's simple, aesthetically gorgeous, and absolutely delicious.

DURATION: 30 minutes

YIELD: 3 to 4 servings

6 cups (1.5 L) vegetable broth

Salt

1⅓ cups (320 g) carnaroli, arborio, or vialone nano rice

¼ cup (60 ml) extra-virgin olive oil

½ large white onion, diced

¾ cup (175 ml) white wine

2 cups (480 ml) Simple Tomato Sauce (page 32)

2 tablespoons (30 g) unsalted butter

3½ ounces (100 g) Parmigiano-Reggiano cheese, grated

1. In a medium pot, warm the broth on the stovetop; it does not need to boil or simmer. The saltiness of the stock is what will season the risotto. Most store-bought broths are already plenty salty, but if using a homemade broth, be sure to salt it to taste.

2. Meanwhile, add the rice to a small skillet and toast over medium-high heat for 2 to 3 minutes, stirring or tossing frequently to avoid burning it. Remove from the heat.

3. Add the olive oil and onion to a large pan or shallow pot (a sauté pan works well) over medium heat. Cook, stirring frequently, until the onion is tender and slightly transparent, 2 to 3 minutes. Add the rice and stir everything together so that the rice can absorb the oil a bit.

4. Pour in the wine, reduce the heat to medium-low, and bring to a simmer. Let simmer until the rice has absorbed almost all the liquid. Add the tomato sauce and use a ladle to spoon in just enough of the warm broth to submerge the rice. Bring the risotto to a gentle simmer. Continue to simmer the rice, stirring occasionally and adding a little more broth as needed, to maintain the liquid in the pan, until the rice is fully cooked; it usually takes 15 to 17 minutes for the rice to reach al dente but consult the recommended cook time on the package and trust your taste. When the rice is about 2 minutes away from reaching al dente, stop adding broth so that the risotto thickens slightly.

5. When the rice is cooked to your taste, take the risotto off the heat and stir in the butter and cheese. Cover the saucepan and let rest for 2 to 3 minutes before serving.

RISOTTO AGLI ASPARAGI

⊱ *Asparagus Risotto* ⊰

This classic risotto has a very delicate, elegant taste, which is probably why it has the reputation of being a go-to dish for a date night or fancy meal. There's nothing fancy about its preparation, though, which is quite simple and easy to master.

DURATION: 30 minutes

YIELD: 3 or 4 servings

8 cups (2 L) vegetable broth

Salt

1⅓ cups (320 g) carnaroli, arborio, or vialone nano rice

3 tablespoons (45 g) unsalted butter, divided

½ large white onion, diced

10½ ounces (300 g) asparagus, trimmed, tips cut off, and stems cut into 1-inch (2.5 cm) pieces

¾ cup (175 ml) white wine

1 tablespoon (15 ml) extra-virgin olive oil

3½ ounces (100 g) Parmigiano-Reggiano cheese, grated, plus more for topping (optional)

1. In a medium pot, warm the broth on the stovetop; it does not need to boil or simmer. The saltiness of the stock is what will season the risotto. Most store-bought broths are already plenty salty, but if using a homemade broth, be sure to salt it to taste.

2. Meanwhile, add the rice to a small skillet and toast over medium-high heat for 2 to 3 minutes, stirring or tossing frequently to avoid burning it. Remove from the heat.

3. In a large pan or shallow pot (a sauté pan works well), add 2 tablespoons (30 g) of the butter and the onion. Cook, stirring frequently, over medium heat until the onion is tender and slightly transparent, 2 to 3 minutes. Add the asparagus stems and cook, stirring occasionally, for an additional 5 minutes. Add the rice and stir everything together until the rice is completely coated in butter.

4. Pour in the wine, reduce the heat to medium-low, and bring to a simmer. Let simmer until the rice has absorbed almost all the liquid. Use a ladle to spoon in just enough of the warm broth to submerge the rice, then bring the risotto to a gentle simmer. Continue to simmer the rice, stirring occasionally and adding a little more broth as needed to maintain the liquid in the pan, until the rice is fully cooked; it usually takes 15 to 17 minutes for the rice to reach al dente but consult the recommended cook time on the package and trust your taste.

5. While the risotto cooks, add the olive oil and asparagus tips to a small skillet and cook, stirring frequently, over medium-high heat until tender. Remove from the heat.

6. When the rice is about 2 minutes away from reaching al dente, stop adding broth so that the risotto thickens slightly. Once the rice is cooked to your taste, turn off the heat. Stir in the asparagus heads, the remaining 1 tablespoon butter, and the grated Parmigiano. Cover the saucepan and let the risotto rest for 2 to 3 minutes before serving.

7. If you like, you can top it with an extra grating of Parmigiano.

RISOTTO CON LA ZUCCA

⇥ *Squash Risotto* ⇤

This recipe holds a very dear place in our hearts, as Eva cooked it a lot during our first few months together when we were living in Maine. In fact, it was one of the first dishes we shared together. Italy has a different selection of squash than what we can find in the United States, but butternut squash works well for this recipe. That being said, most other varieties of winter squash will work too.

DURATION: 45 minutes

YIELD: 3 or 4 servings

8 cups (2 L) vegetable broth

Salt

3 tablespoons (45 g) unsalted butter, divided

½ large onion, diced

1 pound (450 g) butternut squash, peeled and cut into roughly ½-inch (13 mm) pieces

Freshly ground black pepper

1⅓ cups (320 g) carnaroli, arborio, or vialone nano rice

¾ cup (185 ml) white wine

3½ ounces (100 g) Parmigiano-Reggiano cheese, grated

1. In a medium pot, warm the broth on the stovetop; it does not need to boil or simmer. Most store-bought broths are already plenty salty, but if using a homemade broth, be sure to salt it to taste.

2. In a large pan or shallow pot (a sauté pan works well), add 2 tablespoons (30 g) of the butter and the onion, and cook, stirring frequently, over medium-low heat until tender and slightly transparent, 2 to 3 minutes. Stir in the squash and continue to cook, stirring occasionally, for an additional 5 minutes. Season the squash with a pinch each of salt and pepper; add about ¾ cup (180 ml) of the warm broth and bring to a gentle simmer. Let simmer for 10 to 15 minutes, until the squash is tender but not completely soft. Add a little more broth as needed if the liquid evaporates too much to maintain a simmer.

3. Meanwhile, add the rice to a small skillet and toast over high heat for 2 to 3 minutes, stirring or tossing frequently to avoid burning it. Remove from the heat.

4. When the squash is ready, stir in the rice. Pour in the wine, reduce the heat to medium-low, and bring to a simmer. Let simmer until the rice has absorbed almost all the liquid. Ladle in enough broth to cover the rice, then bring to a simmer again. Continue to simmer the rice, stirring occasionally and adding a little more broth as needed to maintain the liquid in the pan, until the rice is fully cooked; it usually takes 15 to 17 minutes for the rice to reach al dente but consult the recommended cook time on the package and trust your taste. When the rice is about 2 minutes away from reaching al dente, stop adding broth so that the risotto thickens slightly.

5. When the rice is cooked to your taste and the consistency of the risotto is creamy but not soupy, turn off the heat. Stir in the remaining 1 tablespoon (15 g) butter and the cheese. Cover the pan and let rest for 2 to 3 minutes before serving.

6. Cover the pan and let the risotto rest for 2 to 3 minutes before serving.

RISI E BISI

↠ *Venetian Rice & Peas* ↞

This dish was invented in Venice during a time when contact with the Arab world left its mark on Italian food. This influence is visible in the traditional risi e bisi (rice and peas) recipe by a notable lack of alcohol. While this dish isn't quite a risotto—it's meant to be a little soupier—it's common today to cook it more like a risotto and include white wine. A real risi e bisi is made with fresh peas, and the pea pods are included in the broth for extra flavor. Fresh peas are almost impossible to find in the United States, so frozen peas are the closest many of us will ever get. While carnaroli or arborio rice will work, it's better to seek out vialone nano rice, which is better suited to the soupy nature of this dish.

DURATION: 30 minutes

YIELD: 3 or 4 servings

---

13 cups (3 L) vegetable broth

Salt (optional)

1⅓ cups (320 g) vialone nano rice

3 tablespoons (45 g) unsalted butter, divided

½ white onion, diced

¾ cup (175 ml) white wine

1½ cups (200 g) frozen peas

1¾ ounces (50 g) Parmigiano-Reggiano cheese, grated

1. In a large pot, warm the broth on the stovetop; it does not need to boil or simmer. Most store-bought broths are already plenty salty, but if using a homemade broth, be sure to salt it to taste.

2. Meanwhile, add the rice to a small skillet and toast it over medium heat for 2 to 3 minutes, stirring or tossing frequently to avoid burning it. Remove from the heat.

3. In a large pan or shallow pot (a sauté pan works well), add 2 tablespoons (30 g) of the butter and the onion. Cook, stirring frequently, over medium heat until the onion is tender and slightly translucent, 2 to 3 minutes. Add the rice and stir everything together until the rice is completely coated in butter.

4. Pour in the wine, reduce the heat to medium-low, and bring to a simmer. Let simmer until the rice has absorbed almost all the liquid, then ladle in enough of the warm broth to submerge the rice. Bring the rice to a gentle simmer again.

5. The cooking process is the same as for a basic risotto: let the rice simmer until it is al dente to your taste (cook as directed by the package directions) while stirring occasionally and adding more broth as necessary to maintain moisture. The only difference is the amount of broth to add; risi e bisi should be quite thin, comparatively, somewhere between a risotto and a soup. After the rice has been cooking for 10 minutes in the broth, stir in the peas.

6. When the rice is al dente, stir in the remaining 1 tablespoon (15 g) butter and the Parmigiano.

7. Serve immediately.

RISOTTO AL SALTO

⤙ *Pan-Fried Leftover Risotto* ⤚

This recipe was created as a way to reuse leftover risotto. If you're like us, you're wondering if leftover risotto even exists. Risotto al salto is so delicious that many Italians whip up a batch of risotto specifically to make it, and we recommend giving it a shot. The concept works with any kind of risotto, so feel free to try the method with your favorite variation.

DURATION: 1 hour, plus overnight resting

YIELD: Depends on the amount of leftover risotto

Leftover risotto

1 to 2 tablespoons (15 to 30 g) unsalted butter, plus more for greasing

1. Let the risotto cool to room temperature, then transfer it to an airtight container and refrigerate overnight.

2. In a nonstick pan (choose a pan that has a lid and can fit the risotto when spread in a roughly ½-inch, or 13-mm, layer), melt the butter over medium heat. Add the cold risotto and flatten it with a spatula to fill the pan.

3. Cook the risotto for 10 to 12 minutes, until the bottom develops a browned crust. To check this, carefully lift a side of the risotto a little bit with a spatula.

4. Lightly grease the pan's lid with butter. Hold the lid tightly on top, then carefully flip the pan upside down so that the risotto now lies on the lid. Gently slide the risotto back into the pan so that the uncooked bottom can brown. Cook for an additional 10 to 12 minutes.

5. To serve, tightly hold a cutting board on top of the pan and carefully flip the risotto one more time so that it rests on the board.

6. Cut into slices and serve warm.

TIMBALLO DI RISO

⇥ *Calabrian Baked Rice* ⇤

There are many versions of baked, stuffed rice in southern Italy, but we've chosen the one closest to home for us. It's a rich, hearty dish that can easily stand in for a lasagna for Sunday lunch, but it's also perfect for taking to a picnic, because rice doesn't need to be eaten hot and fresh like pasta. One can often see baked rice on Calabrian beaches in the summer.

DURATION: 3½ hours

YIELD: 8 servings

---

3 tablespoons (45 ml) extra-virgin olive oil

8 ounces (225 g) ground beef

8 ounces (225 g) ground pork

1 rib celery, diced

½ large carrot, diced

¼ white onion, diced

1 cup (240 ml) red or white wine

28 ounces (800 g) canned whole peeled tomatoes, crushed with a fork or by hand

Salt and freshly ground black pepper

2½ cups (600 g) arborio rice

5 cups (1.2 L) warm water

2 tablespoons (30 g) unsalted butter, plus more for greasing and topping

5½ ounces (150 g) pecorino cheese, grated, divided

Bread crumbs, for dusting

About 3 ounces (85 g) sliced Calabrian salami

5 hard-boiled eggs, sliced

8 ounces (225 g) mozzarella cheese, chopped

1. In a large pot, heat the olive oil pot over medium heat. Add the ground meat and cook until browned, breaking it up into a fine crumble with a wooden spoon as it cooks. Stir in the celery, carrot, and onion and cook, stirring occasionally, for an additional 5 minutes.

2. Add the wine and bring to a simmer. When almost all the excess moisture has evaporated, add the crushed tomatoes and 1½ cups (360 ml) of water. Season with salt and pepper. Reduce the heat to medium-low and let simmer, partially covered, for 1 hour.

3. Add the rice directly to the pot with the warm water. Bring to a simmer over medium-low heat and cook until the rice is al dente to your taste, 15 to 20 minutes, stirring occasionally. Season with salt as it nears completion. The final consistency should be slightly soupier than a risotto; you can thin it with a little more warm water if necessary.

4. Turn off the heat and stir in the butter and about half of the grated pecorino. Preheat the oven to 400°F (205°C).

5. Grease a 3½-quart (3.5 L) lasagna baking dish with butter. Sprinkle a handful of bread crumbs evenly over the bottom. Ladle half of the rice into the dish and spread it evenly. Top the rice with an even layer of salami slices, hard-boiled egg slices, chopped mozzarella, and most of the remaining pecorino (save some for topping). Cover with the remaining rice, spreading it flat from edge to edge.

6. Top the rice with a generous dusting of bread crumbs and the remaining pecorino. Dot the top with a few thin pats of butter.

7. Cover the dish with aluminum foil and bake for 20 minutes. Remove the foil and bake for an additional 15 to 20 minutes, until the top starts to crisp.

8. Let cool for 15 minutes before serving warm, or let it cool completely and serve at room temperature.

SECONDO

⊱ **Second Courses** ⊰

A secondo, or second course, usually means meat or fish, but there are some notable exceptions of vegetarian dishes that are filling enough to be considered secondi (such as Parmigiana di Melanzane on page 144). Slow cooking is a common theme among secondi, with meat or fish typically being roasted or braised to flavorful perfection.

PARMIGIANA DI MELANZANE

⤙ *Eggplant Parmigiana with Tomato Sauce & Mozzarella* ⤚

To make a proper parmigiana, the eggplant must be fried but not breaded—a common mistake. This dish relies on the exquisite interplay between olive oil and eggplants, a process that should not be interrupted by egg, flour, and bread crumbs. One of the biggest frustrations with making a good parmigiana is trying to keep the dish from becoming too wet, a particularly common problem in North America, where eggplants are bred to be as huge and waterlogged as possible. To remedy this, try cooking down the tomato sauce a little bit so that it is thicker and drain the chopped mozzarella overnight in a strainer.

DURATION: 2 to 3 hours, largely unattended

YIELD: 4 to 6 servings

Extra-virgin olive oil, for frying

3 large eggplants (see Note), sliced into thin rounds

Salt

3 cups (720 ml) Simple Tomato Sauce (page 32)

1 pound (450 g) mozzarella cheese, or to taste, chopped

About 12 fresh basil leaves, torn

1 cup (85 g) grated Parmigiano-Reggiano cheese, or to taste

1. Preheat the oven to 400°F (205°C).

2. Fill a large, deep pan with 1 inch (2.5 cm) of olive oil and heat to frying temperature (see How to Fry at Home on page 34). Working in batches so as not to overcrowd the pan, drop in the eggplant slices and fry until they are lightly golden and wrinkled. Remove the slices with a slotted spoon to a paper towel–lined plate to drain, then sprinkle them with salt.

3. Spread a thin layer of tomato sauce in the bottom of a 2-quart (2 L) baking dish. (Depending on the shape of your dish, you should end up with 4 to 6 layers, so divide your ingredients accordingly.) Cover the sauce with a layer of slightly overlapping fried eggplant slices. Over the eggplant, spread some of the mozzarella, some pieces of basil, and a generous grating of Parmigiano. Spread another thin layer of sauce and repeat the layering of the fried eggplant, mozzarella, basil, and Parmigiano until you have used all the eggplant. Finish by covering the top with an even spread of tomato sauce and plenty of grated Parmigiano.

4. Cover the dish with aluminum foil and bake for 30 minutes. Remove the foil and cook for an additional 30 minutes, or until the top begins to brown and crisp.

5. Let cool for at least 30 minutes before serving. The longer the parmigiana rests, the better. We recommend letting it rest for several hours, then reheating it in a warm oven before serving. You can serve it warm or cold.

NOTE *Another option to help prevent your parmigiana from becoming too wet, especially when using eggplants out of season, is to lightly salt both sides of the vegetable slices, stack them in a colander, and place a heavy weight on top. Let them drain for at least 1 hour, preferably 2 to 3 hours. This will draw out a lot of excess moisture and help sweeten the eggplants.*

OSSOBUCO ALLA MILANESE

⇥ *Veal Shanks in White Wine Sauce* ⇤

This classic dish from Milan is made with veal shanks braised in a tangy white wine sauce until fall-off-the-bone tender. It's delicious as is, but for the authentic experience, try serving it atop Risotto alla Milanese (page 129). It's one of the rare instances in Italian cuisine in which a first and second course are served together on the same plate, and for good reason: the pairing is extraordinarily delicious.

DURATION: 2½ hours, largely unattended

YIELD: 2 servings; the cooked veal shanks can be cut in half to serve 4 when paired with a filling risotto

———

4 cups (1 L) beef broth

2 whole cross-cut veal shanks (see Note)

All-purpose flour

¼ cup (60 g) unsalted butter

2 tablespoons (30 ml) extra-virgin olive oil

½ large white onion, diced or thinly sliced

½ cup (120 ml) white wine

Salt

About 2 teaspoons (4 g) grated lemon zest

2 cloves garlic, minced

1 tablespoon (3.5 g) chopped fresh parsley

1. In a large saucepan, bring the broth to a gentle simmer. Meanwhile, prep the veal shanks: in 4 or 5 places around the edges of each shank, slice through the tough ring of surrounding fat with a sharp knife or kitchen shears; this will prevent curling and allow the meat to remain flat as it cooks.

2. Spread flour on a large plate and dust the shanks in it so that the meat is lightly coated on all sides.

3. In a large pan, heat the butter and olive oil over medium heat. When the butter has melted, add the onion and cook, stirring frequently, until tender, 2 to 3 minutes. Use a spoon to remove the onion to a small dish, making sure to drain the butter and oil back into the pan.

4. Lay the veal shanks in the pan and cook them for 1 to 2 minutes, until lightly browned, then flip and cook the other sides. Add the onion back into the pan and distribute it evenly around the meat.

5. Add the wine and bring to a simmer. Let simmer for 1 to 2 minutes, until the smell of alcohol has dissipated. Ladle warm beef broth over the meat until there is about ½ inch (13 mm) of liquid in the pan. Season lightly with salt. Bring this to a gentle simmer and cover the pan.

6. Let simmer for about 2 hours, or until the meat is very tender and nearly falling off the bone. As it cooks, occasionally flip the meat and add more broth as necessary to maintain liquid in the pan. When the meat is nearing completion, stop adding broth so that the sauce can thicken slightly. Taste the sauce and add salt if necessary.

7. Meanwhile, mix the lemon zest, garlic, and parsley together in a small bowl.

8. Serve the veal sprinkled with the lemon-garlic mixture and a drizzle of the pan sauce.

NOTE *While ossobuco is traditionally made with veal, you can try cross-cut beef shanks using the same preparation for an excellent substitute.*

POLLO E PATATE AL FORNO

→| Baked Chicken & Potatoes |←

Italians generally look down on chicken as a protein, preferring fattier meat such as pork or beef. The upside of this pickiness is that while Italy may not produce a lot of chicken recipes, the handful of traditional preparations that do exist must maintain a high level of deliciousness in order to stick around. We love a good pollo alla cacciatora, but the truth is that it's a very regional dish that most Italians outside of Tuscany don't make. Pollo e patate, on the other hand, is the go-to chicken dish throughout Italy.

DURATION: 1½ hours, largely unattended

YIELD: 4 servings

---

28 ounces (800 g) russet potatoes

4 skin-on chicken drumsticks

4 bone-in, skin-on chicken thighs

4 or 5 sprigs fresh rosemary

2 cloves garlic, peeled

Extra-virgin olive oil

Salt and freshly ground black pepper

1. Preheat the oven to 395°F (200°C).

2. Peel the potatoes and cut them into large chunks or wedges (about 1½ inches, or 4 cm, thick).

3. Place them in a baking pan and nestle the chicken pieces among them, along with the rosemary and garlic cloves. Add a generous drizzle of olive oil and sprinkle with salt and pepper. Use your hands to massage the oil and seasoning into the chicken and potatoes so that everything is evenly coated.

4. Cover the pan with aluminum foil and bake for 30 minutes. Remove the foil and cook for an additional 30 minutes, or until the chicken skin is browned and the potatoes are tender and slightly crispy.

5. Serve hot with the chicken and potatoes drizzled in plenty of pan drippings.

POLPETTE AL SUGO

⤙ *Meatballs in Tomato Sauce* ⤚

When it comes to meatballs, every Italian believes that "Mamma does it best." Eva is no exception, so here we have shared the recipe of her mother, Mamma Rosa. The secret to a great Italian meatball is getting the right balance among meat, bread crumbs, cheese, and egg to achieve a texture that is soft and moldable without being sticky. You really need to measure by feel, as the meat and bread can (and will) vary in humidity. There are many ways to cook polpette, but one of the yummiest and simplest is to simmer them in tomato sauce. Not only do the meatballs absorb a ton of flavor and remain moist, but the remaining sauce packs a meaty punch reminiscent of a ragù. Here are a few tips from Mamma Rosa: Use fresh bread crumbs, not dried; you can easily make them by grating some homemade bread that is a day or two old. While you should certainly add a pinch of salt to your meatball mixture, it's best to season it with plenty of finely grated cheese, because you can add as much as you want without risking over-salting the meat. And although Mamma Rosa prefers using only pork, you can also use beef, veal, or any mix of these meats.

DURATION: 1½ hours, largely unattended

YIELD: About fifteen 2-inch (5 cm) meatballs

---

1 pound (450 g) ground pork

1 to 2 cups (150 to 300 g) fresh bread crumbs

1 or 2 large eggs

Grated Parmigiano-Reggiano and/or pecorino cheese

2 tablespoons (7 g) chopped fresh parsley

Salt and freshly ground black pepper

28 ounces (800 g) canned whole peeled tomatoes

1 clove garlic, peeled

¼ cup (60 ml) extra-virgin olive oil

3 or 4 fresh basil leaves

1. In a large bowl, combine the meat with 1 cup (150 g) bread crumbs, 1 egg, a very generous grating of cheese (you really can't have too much), the parsley, and a generous pinch each of salt and pepper. Mix the ingredients thoroughly by hand; the mixture should be soft enough that it can be rolled into very smooth balls but not wet and sticky. If the mixture is too wet, add more bread crumbs; if it is too firm and crumbly, add another egg. When you have a texture you like, scoop up enough meat to roll a 2-inch (5 cm) ball between your palms. Set it aside on a plate and repeat until all the remaining meat has been used.

2. In a large saucepan, combine the tomatoes, garlic clove, olive oil, basil, and a generous pinch of salt with 1 cup (240 ml) of water. Bring to a simmer and let cook for 10 minutes. Mash the whole tomatoes with a fork, then gently add the meatballs to the sauce.

3. Bring the sauce to a simmer again, partially cover the pot, and let the meatballs cook until the sauce has thickened to your liking, up to 1 hour. As they cook, occasionally swirl the pot to turn the meatballs (it's okay if they don't remain completely covered in the sauce). When the sauce is nearing completion, be sure to taste it and season with salt.

4. Serve the meatballs hot with plenty of sauce drizzled on top. (Any remaining sauce can be considered a bonus, supercharged tomato sauce for use elsewhere.)

SALSICCE CON CIME DI RAPA

⤜ *Calabrian Sausages with Broccoli Rabe* ⤛

This Calabrian sausage and broccoli rabe dish couldn't be simpler, and the results couldn't be more surprising. The merging of these two ingredients creates a combined flavor that is unbelievably delicious. It's one of our go-to Calabrian second courses for a reason. You'll want to use a fairly large pot to cook the bulky raw broccoli rabe, although the greens will quickly wilt and reduce in size.

DURATION: 1 hour

YIELD: 3 or 4 servings

4 tablespoons (60 ml) extra-virgin olive oil, divided

2 cloves garlic, peeled

1 dried or fresh chili pepper, chopped

2 pounds (900 g) broccoli rabe

Salt

4 to 6 mild Italian sausages, pierced with a fork or knife

Freshly ground black pepper

½ cup (120 ml) white wine

1. In a large pot, combine 2 tablespoons (30 ml) of the olive oil, the garlic cloves, and the chopped chili pepper over medium heat. When the garlic starts to sizzle, add the broccoli rabe and cover the pot to keep the steam in. Reduce the heat slightly and let cook for 20 to 30 minutes, until the stems are tender, stirring occasionally. Nearing completion, season the greens with salt. Turn off the heat when cooked.

2. Meanwhile, in a separate large pot, heat the remaining 2 tablespoons olive oil over medium-high heat. Add the sausages and cook, turning frequently, for a few minutes until lightly browned on all sides. Season them with salt and pepper, then add the wine. Reduce the heat to medium-low, partially cover the pot, and bring the liquid to a simmer. Braise the sausages for 20 to 30 minutes, until fully cooked through.

3. Add the broccoli rabe and gently stir everything together. Increase the heat to bring to a brisk simmer and let the sausages cook until the liquid has thickened.

4. Serve warm.

BRACIOLE

⊱ *Stuffed Meat Rolls* ⊰

Braciole are rolled-up meat cutlets stuffed with a sweet and savory filling and simmered to perfection in tomato sauce. They may seem a bit odd to the uninitiated, but after trying them, you'll understand why we look forward to having them on Sundays. You can cook braciole by themselves, as we show here, but you can also include them as one of the meats in a Ragù alla Napoletana (page 81). The choice of meat is quite flexible; pork, beef, and veal are the common options. If you're an adventurous cook, try pork skin or pancetta (pork belly). What's important is that the meat is cut very thin so that it can be rolled up nicely. No two cutlets are exactly the same size, so take the ingredient measurements with a grain of salt. Feel free to add or subtract bread, raisins, pine nuts, and/or parsley as needed to adequately cover each piece of meat and fill the rolls.

DURATION: 3 to 4 hours, largely unattended

YIELD: 4 servings

---

4 thin meat (pork, beef, or veal) cutlets (at least 8 inches, or 20 cm, long)

4 slices homemade bread (such as Basic Bread on page 56)

¼ cup (40 g) raisins

¼ cup (40 g) pine nuts

¼ cup (15 g) chopped fresh parsley

4 cloves garlic, diced

Grated Parmigiano-Reggiano or pecorino cheese

Salt and freshly ground black pepper

¼ cup (60 g) extra-virgin olive oil

½ large white onion, diced

½ large carrot, diced

1 rib celery, diced

⅔ cup (150 ml) white wine

28 ounces (800 g) canned whole peeled tomatoes

1. Place each of the meat cutlets between sheets of parchment paper and pound them with a meat tenderizer or rolling pin until they are very thin and flat. Remove the parchment paper.

2. Cut off and discard the crust of 1 slice of bread. Tear the slice into small pieces and distribute it evenly over the surface of a cutlet, leaving about 1 inch (2.5 cm) of meat bare around the edges. On top of the bread, sprinkle 1 tablespoon raisins, 1 tablespoon pine nuts, 1 tablespoon parsley, and 1 diced garlic clove. Finish by seasoning with a generous grating of cheese and a pinch each of salt and pepper. Roll the cutlet up lengthwise, like a carpet. About halfway through rolling, fold the edges in, then finish rolling; it should resemble a small meat burrito. Use butcher's twine to tie the braciola tightly so that it will not unwrap and the ends cannot open. Repeat with the remaining cutlets and fillings.

3. In a medium pot, heat the olive oil over medium heat. Add the onion, carrot, and celery and cook, stirring frequently, until the onion becomes tender and slightly transparent, 2 to 3 minutes. Push the vegetables aside to create space for the meat.

continued on following page >>

4. Add the braciole to the pot and brown on all sides. When the meat is no longer pink, add the wine and bring to a simmer. Let cook until the wine has almost completely evaporated, 20 to 25 minutes.

5. Add the tomatoes, ½ cup (120 ml) of water, and a generous pinch of salt. Bring to a gentle simmer and cook, partially covered, for 1½ to 2 hours, until the sauce has thickened and the meat is very tender. If the sauce thickens too much while cooking, add a little warm water to thin it. Move the braciole around occasionally to keep them from burning on the bottom while they cook. Remove the meat from the sauce and remove and discard the twine.

6. Serve the braciole warm with extra sauce from the pot drizzled on top.

TRIPPA ALLA ROMANA

⊰ *Roman-Style Tripe in Tomato Sauce* ⊱

Sometimes on our food tours of Italy, we stop by a little market stand to sample trippa alla Romana. When our guests learn that tripe is cow stomach, almost all of them swear they won't touch it. It's incredible to see the change when they finally summon the courage to try a bite: they can't stop coming back for more! Long story short, don't write off this strange ingredient. There's a reason it's the very first thing we ask Mamma Rosa to cook when we arrive in Italy!

DURATION: 3½ hours, largely unattended, plus some prep a day in advance

YIELD: 4 or 5 servings

1¼ pounds (1 kg) tripe (see Note), precleaned and cut into roughly 2-inch (5 cm) chunks

1 tablespoon (17 g) baking soda

¼ cup plus 3 tablespoons (105 ml) extra-virgin olive oil

½ large carrot, chopped

1 rib celery, chopped

¼ large onion, chopped

1 whole dried or fresh chili pepper (optional)

3 bay leaves

1 cup (240 ml) white wine

28 ounces (800 g) canned whole peeled tomatoes

Salt and freshly ground black pepper

About 10 fresh mint leaves, torn

1. The day before you plan to serve it, place the tripe in a large bowl and fill it with cold water to cover. Mix in the baking soda and let the tripe soak overnight (no need to refrigerate).

2. The next day, drain the tripe. Bring a large pot of water to a rolling boil, add the tripe, and boil for 20 minutes. Drain the tripe again.

3. In a large pot, heat the olive oil over medium heat. Add the carrot, celery, onion, chili pepper, and bay leaves and cook, stirring frequently, until the onion is tender and slightly transparent, 2 to 3 minutes. Add the tripe and continue to cook, stirring frequently, for an additional 10 minutes.

4. Add the wine and bring to a simmer. Let simmer, stirring occasionally, for 30 minutes, or until most of the liquid has evaporated. Add the tomatoes and a generous sprinkle of salt and pepper. Reduce the heat to medium-low, bring the sauce to a gentle simmer, and let cook for 2 hours, or until the tripe is very tender. If the sauce thickens too much to maintain a simmer, add a little bit of water. As the tripe nears completion, season again with salt.

5. Turn off the heat and stir in the mint.

6. Serve hot.

NOTE *Tripe is available from good butchers and Mexican markets (where it's called* menudo; *don't be confused by* trippa, *which means "intestines" in Spanish). Make sure the tripe is precleaned, which will give it a very white appearance; it shouldn't be gray or brown.*

AGNELLO AL FORNO ALLA LUCANA

Basilicata-Style Roasted Lamb

There are many variations of oven-roasted lamb dishes in Italy, but we've chosen the Basilicata version because of its delicious particularity: a seasoned bread-crumb mixture that thickens and absorbs the pan juices. Here, we've presented a recipe using rib and loin chops, but just about any cut of lamb will work, provided it's butchered into medium-size pieces.

DURATION: 2 hours, largely unattended, plus overnight marinating

YIELD: 4 to 6 servings

2 pounds (900 g) lamb loin chops

2 pounds (900 g) lamb rib chops

2 large onions, divided

1 tablespoon whole black peppercorns

1 sprig fresh rosemary

1 sprig fresh thyme

5 fresh sage leaves

4 bay leaves

1 bottle (750 ml) red wine

4 tablespoons (60 ml) extra-virgin olive oil, divided

28 ounces (800 g) small roasting potatoes

Salt

1⅓ cups (100 g) bread crumbs

3½ ounces (100 g) pecorino cheese, grated

1 clove garlic, minced

1 tablespoon (3.5 g) chopped fresh parsley, or to taste

9 ounces (250 g) cherry tomatoes, cut in half

Freshly ground black pepper

1. Place the meat in a large bowl. Cut one of the onions into quarters and add it to the bowl with the peppercorns, rosemary, thyme, sage, and bay leaves. Add the bottle of red wine, taking care to ensure that the lamb is mostly covered. Cover the bowl with plastic wrap or a lid and marinate in the refrigerator overnight.

2. Preheat the oven to 450°F (230°C). Drain the marinated lamb and pat the meat dry with a paper towel. Grease the bottom of a large roasting pan with 2 tablespoons (30 ml) of the olive oil.

3. Spread the meat evenly in the pan. Cut the remaining onion into thick slices. Fill the gaps around the meat with the onion slices and the whole potatoes. Generously salt the meat.

4. In a large bowl, combine the bread crumbs, pecorino, garlic clove, parsley, cherry tomatoes, and a pinch each of salt and pepper and mix well. Evenly sprinkle this mixture over the lamb and potatoes. Drizzle the remaining 2 tablespoons (30 ml) olive oil over everything.

5. Cover the pan with aluminum foil and bake for 45 minutes. Remove the foil and bake for an additional 20 to 25 minutes, until the bread crumbs become slightly crispy and the juices have thickened.

6. Serve hot.

POLPETTONE

⊰ *Stuffed Meatloaf* ⊱

Italians call meatloaf *polpettone*, which literally means "big meatball." Anyone who is familiar with making Italian meatballs (see Polpette al Sugo on page 149) will recognize the similar method behind the meat mixture for a polpettone. Because the moisture in meat varies substantially, this process is an art more than a science: you need to use your senses when creating the perfect balance of meat, cheese, bread crumbs, and eggs—not too sticky (add more bread crumbs), not too dry and crumbly (add another egg).

DURATION: 1½ hours

YIELD: 6 servings

---

1 pound (450 g) ground beef

2 ounces (55 g) Parmigiano-Reggiano cheese, grated

2 ounces (55 g) pecorino cheese, grated

1 cup (130 g) bread crumbs, plus more if needed

4 or 5 large eggs

Salt and freshly ground black pepper

3½ ounces (100 g) prosciutto cotto or ham, thinly sliced

3½ ounces (100 g) provola or provolone cheese, thinly sliced

3 hard-boiled eggs, sliced (optional)

3 or 4 large russet potatoes, peeled and cubed

1 large onion, sliced

15 cherry tomatoes, cut in half

Dried oregano

¼ cup (60 ml) extra-virgin olive oil

3 or 4 sprigs fresh rosemary

2 cloves garlic, peeled

1½ cups (360 ml) white wine, divided, plus more if needed

1. In a large bowl, combine the ground meat, grated cheeses, bread crumbs, and 4 eggs with a generous sprinkle of salt and pepper and mix well; the mixture should be soft and moldable but not too wet or sticky. If it is on the sticky side, add some more bread crumbs to help soak up the moisture; if the meat is a little dry and crumbly, mix in another egg.

2. Tear off a large sheet of parchment paper (about 24 inches, or 60 cm, in length). Transfer the meat mixture onto the parchment and press it flat into a large rectangle that fills the paper, leaving a 2-inch (5 cm) border of paper around the edges.

3. On top of the meat, arrange a layer of prosciutto cotto, followed by a layer of sliced cheese. Evenly distribute the sliced hard-boiled eggs over the cheese.

4. Using the parchment paper to help lift the edges, roll the meat up widthwise; the result should be a long, rolled sausage of ground meat. Press the ends and edge of the roll shut so that the meat completely seals in the filling. Wrap the meat in the parchment paper and twist the ends of the paper closed, like a candy wrapper.

5. Preheat the oven to 485°F (250°C). Combine the potatoes, onion, and cherry tomatoes in a large roasting pan and sprinkle with salt, pepper, and oregano. Drizzle with the olive oil, then thoroughly mix everything together.

continued on following page >>

6. Making space among the vegetables, place the parchment-wrapped meatloaf in the center of the pan. Place the rosemary sprigs and garlic cloves in the pan as well. Pour 1 cup (240 ml) of the wine into the pan and cover with aluminum foil.

7. Bake for 25 minutes, then remove from the oven. Remove the foil (but save it) and carefully unwrap the meat and discard the parchment. Stir the vegetables and baste the meatloaf with the pan juices. If there is little or no liquid in the bottom of the pan, add the remaining ½ cup (120 ml) wine.

8. Cover the pan with foil again and bake for an additional 15 minutes. Remove the foil, stir the vegetables, and baste the meat. If the vegetables are dry, add a little bit more wine to maintain moisture. Bake for 15 to 20 minutes, until the polpettone is lightly browned on top and the potatoes are tender and beginning to crisp.

9. Cut into slices and serve warm with the vegetables from the pan on top.

ORATA ALL'ACQUA PAZZA

⤞ *Sea Bream with Cherry Tomatoes* ⤝

Acqua pazza—literally "crazy water"—is a simple but delicious sauce that is most often paired with whole fish, such as sea bream *(orata)*. Sea bass, mackerel, branzino, cod, and halibut are also good options. Leftover acqua pazza sauce is fantastic with pasta. You can easily add a few extra tomatoes and a little more wine, set aside the fish when cooked, and mix some al dente pasta directly in the pan for a delicious first course.

DURATION: 45 minutes

YIELD: 2 servings; the cooked fish can be filleted to serve 4 when paired with a first course

---

¼ cup (60 ml) extra-virgin olive oil

2 cloves garlic, peeled

12 to 15 cherry tomatoes, cut in half

2 whole sea breams, cleaned and gutted

⅔ cup (160 ml) white wine

Salt and freshly ground black pepper

Chopped fresh parsley, for garnishing

1. In a large pan, heat the olive oil and garlic over medium-high heat. When the garlic starts to sizzle, add the tomatoes and cook, stirring occasionally, until they begin to soften and release their juices, about 5 minutes.

2. Spread the tomatoes to the edges of the pan and lay the fish flat in the center. Add the wine and a generous sprinkle of salt and pepper. Bring to a brisk simmer and cook for a few minutes, until the smell of alcohol dissipates.

3. Reduce the heat to low, cover the pan, and let cook for 20 to 25 minutes, until the fish meat is white and very tender.

4. Serve warm topped with extra sauce from the pan and a sprinkle of chopped parsley.

SALTIMBOCCA ALLA ROMANA

⊰| *Veal Cutlets with Prosciutto & Sage* |⊱

For meat lovers, this dish has it all: it tastes like a million bucks, it's quick and easy to make, and it's surprisingly light for a meal that rivals steak in rich flavor. We often joke that anyone can look forward to a diet with saltimbocca in their arsenal. If you really want to wow someone with unbeatable flavor and presentation in a hurry, this is hard dish to top. The recipe can easily be scaled up, just keep in mind that most pans can only fit about two servings at a time. To cook a larger quantity, either use a very large pan, use multiple pans at once, or cook the cutlets in batches.

DURATION: 45 minutes

YIELD: 2 servings

2 large veal cutlets (about ½ pound, or 225 g, total)

4 slices (30 g) prosciutto crudo

4 fresh sage leaves

All-purpose flour

2 tablespoons (30 g) unsalted butter

¼ cup (60 ml) white wine

Salt and freshly ground black pepper

1. Place each cutlet between sheets of parchment paper and pound them very thin with a meat tenderizer or rolling pin. (If using two 4-ounce, or 115-g, cutlets, cut each one in half lengthwise for a total of 4 meat slices).

2. Lay a slice of prosciutto and a sage leaf on top of each cutlet. Use a toothpick, threaded through twice like a safety pin, to pin all the ingredients together.

3. Place flour on a plate, then dust each cutlet in the flour so that it is lightly coated on both sides.

4. In a large pan, melt the butter over medium heat. Place the veal cutlets, prosciutto sides up, in the pan, and cook, flipping occasionally, for about 5 minutes, or until lightly browned on each side.

5. Add the wine and bring to a simmer. Continue to cook until the liquid has thickened. Sprinkle with salt and pepper.

6. Serve with any remaining pan juices on top. Keep the toothpicks in for presentation but be sure to warn diners.

COSTOLETTA ALLA MILANESE

⊰ *Fried Veal Chops* ⊱

Often confused with cotoletta alla Milanese (*cotoletto* meaning "cutlet"), the original costoletta uses a bone-in veal chop instead of a boneless cutlet. We prefer this version, as the bone helps retain juices in the meat, preventing it from drying out. Often a bone-in veal chop comes with quite a bit of meat along the bone. For the best result, trim off all the excess meat and fat on the bone, up until the point where the bone enters the round chop.

DURATION: 30 minutes

YIELD: 2 servings

---

2 bone-in veal chops, about 1 inch (2.5 cm) thick

2 large eggs

Dried bread crumbs

10 ounces (340 g) clarified butter (see Note), or enough to fill your pan with about 1 inch (2.5 cm) when melted

Salt

Lemon wedges, for serving (optional)

1. In 3 or 4 spots around the edge of each veal chop, cut a small incision with kitchen shears; these cuts will help the meat keep from curling while frying. Place a veal chop beneath sheets of parchment paper and pound it with a meat tenderizer until it is at least half as thin as it was originally. Repeat with the other chop.

2. In a small bowl, whisk the eggs until beaten, then transfer them to a large, rimmed plate. Fill another plate with bread crumbs. Dip each chop first in the eggs, coating them completely, then dredge them thoroughly in the bread crumbs to coat the entire meat surface. Press the bread crumbs into the veal so they adhere well.

3. In a large pan, melt the clarified butter over medium-high heat and bring up to frying temperature (see How to Fry at Home on page 34). Cooking the chops one at a time, carefully lay a chop in the pan and fry for 3 minutes per side, or until golden. As the chop fries, use a spoon to constantly baste the topside with clarified butter.

4. Remove the chops to a paper towel–lined plate and liberally sprinkle with salt.

5. Serve hot with lemon wedges (if using).

NOTE *While you can (and many Italians do) fry the veal in extra-virgin olive oil, the more traditional choice in Milan is clarified butter. Northern Italy is much more prone to using butter over olive oil, and clarified butter (or ghee) is much better suited for frying.*

CARNE ALLA PIZZAIOLA

⋊ *Beef Cutlets Braised in Tomato Sauce* ⋉

Carne alla pizzaiola, which translates to "pizza maker–style meat," is more of a technique than a specific recipe, as it can be applied to just about any thin cutlet. Beef is the most common choice, but pork, chicken breast, and veal are also excellent options. Because the tomato sauce keeps the meat moist and tender, this is a great way to turn lean, cheap cuts into a delicious dish.

DURATION: 20 to 30 minutes

YIELD: 2 servings

3 tablespoons (45 g) extra-virgin olive oil

4 thin beef cutlets

1 clove garlic, thinly sliced

Generous pinch of dried oregano

14 ounces (400 g) canned whole peeled tomatoes, crushed with a fork

Salt

1. In a large pan, heat the olive oil over medium-high heat. Lay the cutlets flat in the pan and cook for about 1 minute on each side, or until they are no longer pink.

2. Add the garlic, oregano, and tomatoes. Reduce the heat to medium, bring the sauce to a simmer, and salt it lightly. Cover the pan and let the meat cook for 15 to 20 minutes, until very tender. Season again with salt. For a thicker sauce, remove the meat from the pan, turn up the heat, and let the tomatoes reduce a bit before serving.

3. Serve the meat hot topped with plenty of sauce.

SPEZZATINO CON LE PATATE

⇥ *Beef & Potato Stew* ⇤

There are as many variations of this stew as there are Italians (maybe more), but all of them follow a similar preparation. We've chosen to share Mamma Rosa's recipe, a prized family possession, which includes the typical Calabrian addition of a chili pepper and some oregano. Some version of this stew can be found on any Italian table—from the north to the south.

DURATION: 3 hours, largely unattended

YIELD: 4 servings

5 tablespoons (75 ml) extra-virgin olive oil

1 large red onion, thinly sliced

1 pound (900 g) beef stew meat, cut into large chunks

1 whole fresh chili pepper (optional)

Salt

1 cup (240 ml) white wine

14 ounces (400 g) whole peeled tomatoes, crushed with a fork

1 cup (240 ml) warm water

Dried oregano

2 large russet potatoes, peeled and cut into 1-inch-thick (2.5 cm) wedges

1. In a large pot, combine the olive oil and onion over medium heat and cook, stirring frequently, until tender and slightly transparent, 2 to 3 minutes. Add the beef chunks and brown them on all sides. Add the whole chili pepper (if using) and a pinch of salt.

2. Continue to cook the beef until any liquid it may have released evaporates. Add the wine, reduce the heat to medium-low, and let simmer for 20 minutes.

3. Stir in the crushed tomatoes and warm water. Season with oregano and a pinch of salt, then let simmer over low heat, partially covered, for 1½ hours, until you can easily insert a fork into the meat. If the stew thickens too much, add a little bit of warm water.

4. Stir the potato wedges into the stew and let simmer, occasionally stirring gently, for an additional 45 minutes, or until both the meat and potatoes are tender. As the stew nears completion, salt it again to taste.

5. Serve warm.

PESCE SPADA ALLA SICILIANA

⊰ *Sicilian Swordfish Steaks* ⊱

During spring, the beaches of southern Italy are packed with brightly colored fishing dories, outfitted for catching swordfish. You can't go a day in the villages without hearing the local fishmonger wailing "Pesce spada! Pesce spada!" over a crackling megaphone. This dish is a classic Sicilian preparation for swordfish steak.

DURATION: 20 to 30 minutes

YIELD: 4 servings

¼ cup (40 g) raisins

3 to 4 tablespoons extra-virgin olive oil

1 clove garlic, peeled

2 anchovies

20 pitted Kalamata olives, cut in half

1 tablespoon (15 g) capers

12 ounces (350 g) cherry tomatoes, cut in half

1 tablespoon (10 g) pine nuts

1 tablespoon (15 ml) warm water

Pinch of dried oregano

Pinch of freshly ground black pepper

4 swordfish steaks (1 inch, or 2.5 cm, thick), or two 2-inch-thick (5 cm) steaks cut in half horizontally (see Note)

Salt

¼ cup (60 ml) white wine

Fresh chopped parsley, for garnishing

1. Place the raisins in a small bowl of water to soak while you begin cooking the sauce.

2. In a large pan, heat the oil and garlic over medium heat. When the garlic starts to sizzle, reduce the heat to medium-low, add the anchovies, and stir until they dissolve in the oil. Increase the heat to medium again, add the olives and capers, and cook, stirring frequently, for 2 to 3 minutes. Add the tomatoes, pine nuts, drained raisins, and warm water to the pan and bring to a simmer.

3. Season the sauce with the oregano and pepper, then continue to simmer until the tomatoes soften and release all their juices. If the sauce dries out, add a little warm water as needed to keep the tomatoes simmering.

4. Lay the swordfish steaks on top of the sauce and generously sprinkle them with salt. Add the wine to the pan and bring to a simmer again. After about 3 minutes, flip the steaks and salt the other sides. Cover the pan and let cook for 10 minutes. Remove the steaks from the pan and let rest.

5. Season the sauce with salt, increase the heat to medium-high, and let it thicken to your liking.

6. Serve the swordfish with the sauce and tomatoes drizzled on top and garnished with chopped parsley.

NOTE *Swordfish steaks are usually cut quite thin in Italy, about 1 inch (2.5 cm) thick. We usually find them about twice as thick in the United States, so for this recipe we've sliced 2 thick, 20-ounce (565 g) steaks in half for 4 servings.*

BRASATO DI MANZO AL VINO ROSSO

⊰ *Roast Beef in Red Wine Sauce* ⊱

One of the advantages of the Italian penchant for slow-braising meat is that leaner, more economical cuts of meat can be transformed into stunning dishes without drying out. Such is the case with brasato di manzo, Italy's answer to roast beef. It works well with tougher beef cuts, such as eye of round roast. We recommend serving this dish with polenta, which soaks up the extra yummy sauce.

DURATION: 3½ to 4 hours, largely unattended

YIELD: 4 to 6 servings

5 tablespoons (75 ml) extra-virgin olive oil

2 pounds (900 g) eye of round beef roast, tied up with butcher's twine

1 large white onion, thinly sliced

3 bay leaves

1 sprig fresh rosemary

5 fresh sage leaves

Salt

2 cups (480 ml) red wine

½ cup (120 ml) tomato passata (puree)

1. In a large pot, heat the olive oil over medium-high for 1 minute, then add the beef and brown on all sides. Add the onion, bay leaves, rosemary, sage, and a sprinkle of salt. Continue to cook for about 10 minutes, stirring frequently, until the onion is tender.

2. Add the wine, tomato passata, and a generous pinch of salt. Reduce the heat to low and let simmer, covered, for 3 hours, or until the meat is tender. For a thicker sauce, remove the lid for the last 20 minutes of cooking.

3. Let the roast rest for 5 minutes. Remove the butcher's twine and thinly slice the meat against the grain.

4. Serve warm with plenty of sauce on top.

POLPO ALLA LUCIANA

✢| *Neapolitan Octopus in Tomato Sauce with Crusty Bread* |✢

This is a dish that we always look for when we visit Naples. Not only is the octopus tender and delicious, but the sauce is so yummy that we usually have to ask for a second round of toasted bread to soak up every last drop.

DURATION: 2 hours, largely unattended

YIELD: 4 servings

¼ cup (60 ml) extra-virgin olive oil

1 clove garlic, peeled

Red chili pepper flakes (optional)

2 whole octopuses (about 24 ounces, or 700 g, total)

½ cup (120 ml) white wine

20 pitted Kalamata olives

1 tablespoon (12 g) capers

17½ ounces (500 g) canned whole peeled tomatoes

½ tablespoon (3.5 g) chopped parsley

Salt and freshly ground black pepper

Toasted bread, for serving (optional, but highly recommended)

1. In a large, deep sauté pan, heat the olive oil, garlic, and a sprinkle of chili pepper flakes (if using) over medium-low heat until the garlic begins to sizzle. Lay the octopuses flat in the pan, reduce the heat to low, and cover. Let cook for 15 minutes.

2. Add the wine and bring to a gentle simmer. Let the octopuses cook, still covered, until fork-tender, about 30 minutes.

3. Add the olives, capers, tomatoes, parsley, a light sprinkle of salt and pepper, and a few spoonfuls of warm water. Bring to a simmer again and cook, covered, for 1 hour, or until the octopuses are very tender. The sauce should have enough liquid to maintain a gentle simmer. If it thickens too much, add a little bit more water. As the dish nears completion, season it with salt, remove the lid, and let the sauce thicken to your liking.

4. Cut each octopus in half and serve hot with some toasted bread for soaking up the extra sauce.

CALAMARI RIPIENI

⤙ *Squid Stuffed with Bread Crumbs & Cheese* ⤚

Calamari Fritti (page 53) is a must-try classic, but it's not the only way Italians prepare squid. If you're looking to turn calamari into a larger, more filling meal, give this stuffed version a shot. Sometimes squid comes pre-sliced for frying. In this case, seek out whole calamari. It's fine if the tentacles are separated (you still want them, though), but the bodies must be intact.

DURATION: 1½ hours

YIELD: 10 calamari; 3 to 5 servings

---

10 whole squid (about 2¼ pounds, or 1 kg), cleaned, with tentacles separated

1¼ cups (160 g) bread crumbs

3½ ounces (100 g) pecorino cheese, grated

1 tablespoon (3.5 g) chopped fresh parsley, plus more for topping

3 cloves garlic, diced, divided

5 tablespoons (75 ml) extra-virgin olive oil, divided

Salt and freshly ground black pepper

½ cup (120 ml) white wine

8 cherry tomatoes, cut in half

1. Dice the squid tentacles, then place in a large bowl.

2. Add the bread crumbs, pecorino, parsley, 2 diced garlic cloves, 3 tablespoons (45 ml) of the olive oil, and a pinch each of salt and pepper. Mix thoroughly.

3. Fill the squid bodies with the stuffing mixture. The calamari should be plump and full but not bursting, as the stuffing will expand when cooked. Securely close the calamari by threading a toothpick through the opening of the cavity in two places, like fastening a safety pin. (You can break off the protruding toothpick ends for a cleaner profile.)

4. In a large pan, heat the remaining 2 tablespoons (30 ml) olive oil over medium-low heat. Add the stuffed calamari and cook for about 2 minutes, turning frequently, to cook evenly on all sides.

5. Add the wine and bring to a simmer. Once the smell of alcohol has dissipated (after about 2 minutes), add the tomatoes, 1 or 2 tablespoons of water, and a sprinkle of salt. Reduce the heat to medium-low and bring to a gentle simmer, partially covered. Let cook for 25 minutes, turning the calamari occasionally. The tomatoes and calamari should release plenty of liquid to maintain a simmer, but if the sauce evaporates, add a little more water.

6. Serve hot topped with tomatoes from the pan and some chopped parsley.

CONTORNO

⊰ **Side Dishes** ⊱

*Every good meal needs a suitable side dish.
Usually, contorni are made with vegetables
that are cooked and served simply. Don't let the
simplicity fool you into underestimating these
dishes, which can be delicious enough to risk
overshadowing a main course.*

PEPERONATA

⊱ *Bell Peppers in Tomato Sauce* ⊰

This is a delicious and simple vegetable side dish that should be served cold, ideally after having sat in the refrigerator overnight. It's a great recipe to make in advance if you have a meal coming up in which you won't have much time to cook something hot.

DURATION: 1½ hours, largely unattended (best made a day in advance)

YIELD: 4 servings

---

4 large bell peppers (red and/or yellow ones look best)

3 tablespoons (45 ml) extra-virgin olive oil

¼ large onion, thinly sliced

14 ounces (400 g) canned whole peeled tomatoes, crushed with a fork or by hand

Salt and freshly ground black pepper

1. Preheat the oven to 400°F (205°C). Line a baking sheet with parchment paper or aluminum foil.

2. Place the whole peppers on the baking sheet and bake for 30 to 40 minutes, until the skins are browned, wrinkled, and loosened. Turn them occasionally as they bake so that they brown evenly.

3. Meanwhile, in a large saucepan, combine the olive oil and onion over medium heat and cook, stirring frequently, until tender and slightly transparent, 2 to 3 minutes. Add the tomatoes and season the sauce generously with salt and pepper. Partially cover the saucepan, bring the tomatoes to a very low simmer, and let cook for about 45 minutes, stirring occasionally. If the sauce thickens too much and risks burning, add a little more water as necessary; the sauce should be quite thick in the end, so do not overdo the added water.

4. As soon as the peppers have finished baking, place them in a paper bag for 10 to 15 minutes; the skins should come off easily after steaming in the bag. Peel the peppers, remove the stems and seeds, and cut them into 1-inch-wide (2.5 cm) strips.

5. Stir the pepper strips into the tomato sauce. Bring to a simmer and cook until the peppers are very tender and the sauce becomes quite thick, 30 to 40 more minutes. Check the salt again and season to taste.

6. Let the dish cool completely before serving (it's ideal to refrigerate overnight and serve it the next day).

POMODORI ARROSTO

⤞ *Baked Tomatoes* ⤝

Like every recipe involving tomatoes, this one is best made with very fresh produce. However, the technique behind this simple side dish is a good trick for making the most out of some tomatoes that maybe aren't quite in season. That's why this is a go-to for us when we're craving some pomodori, but our local grocery store is only carrying some Roma tomatoes that are a bit on the bland side. It works with any kind of tomato, though, from grape tomatoes to big, beautiful heirlooms. It's also a very easy and hands-off recipe that scales up well, so it's perfect if you need a side dish for a big group and have your hands full with the mains.

DURATION: 2 hours, largely unattended

YIELD: 6 to 8 servings

---

15 Roma tomatoes

3 cloves garlic, finely chopped

Dried oregano

Salt and freshly ground black pepper

Extra-virgin olive oil

1. Preheat the oven to 400°F (205°C). Line a baking sheet with parchment paper.

2. Cut the tomatoes in half lengthwise and arrange them on the prepared baking sheet, skin sides down.

3. Top each tomato half with a pinch each of chopped garlic, oregano, salt, pepper, and a generous drizzle of olive oil.

4. Bake for 1 hour and 30 minutes, or until they are very tender. Let cool to room temperature before serving.

CAPONATA DI MELANZANE

✦ *Sicilian Sweet-&-Sour Eggplant Caponata* ✦

Arab conquerors made their mark on Sicilian food with sugar. This dish is the perfect example of a very common Sicilian flavor profile: sweet and sour. Eggplant caponata has a rich, complex taste with lots of delicious surprises. It's best left to refrigerate overnight before serving, but you may have a hard time waiting that long.

DURATION: 1½ hours

YIELD: 3 or 4 servings

¼ cup (40 g) raisins

3 to 4 tablespoons (45 to 60 ml) extra-virgin olive oil, plus more for frying

1 large eggplant, chopped into ½-inch (13 mm) cubes

¼ cup (40 g) pine nuts

½ red onion, thinly sliced

2 ribs celery, chopped

10 to 15 large pitted green olives (Kalamata olives also work well), cut in half

2 tablespoons (25 g) capers

4 ripe vine tomatoes, cut into quarters

Salt and freshly ground black pepper

¼ cup (60 ml) white wine vinegar

1½ tablespoons (20 g) granulated sugar

1 tablespoon tomato paste

About 6 fresh basil leaves, torn

1. Soak the raisins in a small bowl of water while you fry the eggplant.

2. Fill a large, deep pan with about 3 inches (7.5 ml) of olive oil and heat to frying temperature (see How to Fry at Home on page 34). Working in batches so as not to overcrowd the pan, carefully drop the eggplant cubes into the oil and fry, stirring frequently, until they are lightly browned on all sides. Remove with a slotted spoon to a paper towel–lined plate to drain.

3. Add the pine nuts to a small skillet and toast over medium-high heat for 1 to 2 minutes, stirring or tossing constantly to avoid burning them. Set aside. Drain the soaked raisins.

4. Add the 3 to 4 tablespoons (45 to 60 ml) olive oil and the onion to a large skillet over medium heat and cook, stirring frequently, until the onion is tender and slightly translucent. Add the celery, olives, capers, raisins, and toasted pine nuts and cook, stirring frequently, for about 10 minutes.

5. Stir in the tomatoes and season the sauce with salt and pepper. Reduce the heat to medium-low, cover the pan, and cook at a gentle simmer for about 30 minutes, stirring occasionally. Add a little bit of water if the caponata dries out too much and risks burning. Meanwhile, combine the vinegar, sugar, and tomato paste in a small bowl or measuring cup and stir together.

6. Add the vinegar mixture to the pan, increase the heat to medium-high, bring the caponata to a brisk simmer, and stir everything together. Cook for 2 to 3 minutes and season with salt as it cooks. If you desire, you can pick out and discard the tomato skins.

7. Remove the pan from the heat. Stir in the fried eggplant and basil.

8. Let the caponata cool completely before serving.

VERDURE GRATINATE

→| Breaded Baked Vegetables |←

This is a great way to take vegetables to a new level with some simple ingredients you probably have at home right now. We've given instructions for making a mix of different vegetables, but you can easily use this same technique with any produce you like, provided it can be adequately flattened and baked.

DURATION: 1 hour, largely unattended

YIELD: 3 or 4 servings

---

1 tablespoon (15 ml) extra-virgin olive oil, plus more for drizzling

1 medium eggplant

2 large bell peppers

2 large zucchini

Salt and freshly ground black pepper

½ cup (65 g) bread crumbs

1¾ ounces (50 g) Parmigiano-Reggiano cheese, or to taste, grated

1 clove garlic, minced

3 or 4 sprigs fresh parsley, chopped

1. Preheat the oven to 390°F (200°C). Line two baking sheets with parchment paper and drizzle them with olive oil.

2. Cut the eggplant into ¼-inch-thick (6 mm) strips. Cut the bell peppers in half, remove the seeds, and then flatten the halves as much as possible with your palm. Cut the zucchini either into ¼-inch-thick (6 mm) strips or rounds.

3. Arrange the vegetables flat on the baking sheets and score each piece with 3 or 4 shallow knife incisions. Season them generously with salt, pepper, and a drizzle of olive oil. Bake for 30 minutes.

4. Meanwhile, in a medium bowl, combine the bread crumbs, Parmigiano, garlic, 1 tablespoon (15 ml) olive oil, chopped parsley and a generous pinch each of salt and pepper and mix well.

5. When the vegetables are done cooking, remove them from the oven and increase the temperature to 400°F (205°C). Cover each of the vegetable pieces with the bread-crumb mixture, then drizzle them with olive oil. Bake the breaded vegetables for 10 to 15 additional minutes, until they are browned on top, and your kitchen starts to smell amazing.

6. Serve warm.

VERDURE GRIGLIATE

⇥ *Simple Grilled Vegetables* ⇤

This is a very simple and common preparation for a variety of vegetables. We've used eggplant, zucchini, and bell peppers, but feel free to grill what you prefer. Indoors, a heavy grill pan will provide the characteristic grill marks. Otherwise, a cast-iron pan works well. Even better if you can grill the vegetables outdoors over an open flame.

DURATION: 1 hour

YIELD: 3 or 4 servings

1 large bell pepper

1 large zucchini, cut into either rounds or strips (about ¼ inch, or 6 mm, thick)

1 medium eggplant, cut into either rounds or strips (about ¼ inch, or 6 mm, thick)

Extra-virgin olive oil

Salt and freshly ground black pepper

1. Heat a heavy cast-iron grill pan over high heat on the stovetop. Grill the whole pepper, turning it frequently with tongs until the skin has blistered and is charred on all sides. Place the pepper in a paper bag for 15 minutes. (The skin should come off easily after steaming in the bag.)

2. Meanwhile, working in batches, grill the zucchini and eggplant slices in the same pan over high heat on the stovetop for 3 to 4 minutes on each side, or until charred. Remove to a plate.

3. Peel the skin from the pepper, remove the stem and seeds, and cut it into thin strips.

4. Serve the vegetables warm or cold with a drizzle of olive oil and a sprinkle of salt and pepper.

ASPARAGI ALLA PARMIGIANA

✦ *Cheesy Baked Asparagus* ✦

This recipe is as old as the concept of "Italian food" itself, as it comes directly from Pellegrino Artusi's *La scienza in cucina e l'arte di mangiar bene*, the first general Italian cookbook, originally published in 1891. It perfectly adheres to a common Italian approach to vegetables: pairing them with plenty of bread crumbs and Parmigiano-Reggiano cheese.

DURATION: 1 hour

YIELD: 3 or 4 servings

Salt

1 pound (450 g) asparagus, trimmed

About 2 tablespoons (30 g) unsalted butter

Freshly ground black pepper

Parmigiano-Reggiano cheese

¼ cup (35 g) bread crumbs

1. Bring a large pot of water to a rolling boil and salt it generously. Meanwhile, prepare an ice bath in a large bowl.

2. Add the asparagus to the boiling water and blanch for 3 to 4 minutes, then plunge the spears in the prepared ice bath to stop them from cooking. Drain completely.

3. Preheat the oven to 400°F (205°C).

4. Line the bottom of a small baking dish with a few very thin pats of the butter. (We like to use a meatloaf dish, as it's long enough to hold an asparagus spear and narrow enough to allow for multiple layers, but you can also cook them in a flat layer on a larger baking sheet.) Arrange a flat layer of asparagus, side by side, over the butter. Top the asparagus with a sprinkle of pepper, a few more very thin pats of butter, and a thick grating of Parmigiano.

5. Place another layer of asparagus on top and repeat with the pepper, butter, and cheese. Repeat until you have used all the asparagus and it is the top layer.

6. In a small bowl, mix together the bread crumbs with an equal amount of Parmigiano. Evenly spread this mixture on the top asparagus layer. (Note: If you use a large dish with only 1 or 2 layers, you will need more bread crumbs to cover.) Top with some more very thin butter pats.

7. Bake for 20 to 30 minutes, until the asparagus is tender and the bread crumbs are crispy and golden.

8. Serve warm.

ZUCCA IN AGRODOLCE

⇥ *Pan-Fried Sweet-&-Sour Squash* ⇤

Agrodolce roughly translates to "sweet and sour." This flavor profile is very common in Sicilian kitchens, usually combining tart vinegar with sugar. This is one of our favorite squash recipes, and it is always a big hit among guests who try it with us in southern Italy.

DURATION: 40 minutes, plus 3 hours chilling (best made a day in advance)

YIELD: 4 servings

½ large butternut squash (about 21 ounces, or 600 g, after the prep in step 1)

Extra-virgin olive oil, for frying (in this case, EVOO is a must)

Salt and freshly ground black pepper

About 12 fresh mint leaves

1 clove garlic, chopped

¼ cup (60 ml) white wine vinegar

2 tablespoons (30 g) granulated sugar, or to taste

1. Peel the squash and cut it into ½-inch-thick (13 mm) slices. (The shape and length of the slices don't matter.)

2. Fill a large pan with about ½ inch (13 mm) of olive oil and heat over medium-high heat. Working in batches, fry the squash slices on both sides until lightly browned and tender, about 5 minutes total. Remove to a rimmed plate or shallow casserole dish and arrange flat. (The dish can be any shape or size, as long as the squash can comfortably marinate in the sweet-and-sour sauce.)

3. Sprinkle the squash with salt, pepper, mint, and garlic. Drizzle with about ½ cup (120 ml) of olive oil from the pan.

4. Make a dressing by thoroughly mixing together the vinegar and sugar in a small bowl. Pour the dressing evenly over the squash to saturate and soak the slices.

5. Cover with a lid or plastic wrap and let the squash marinate in the refrigerator for at least 3 to 4 hours, or preferably overnight, before serving.

6. Serve at room temperature.

FAGIOLINI ALLA PUGLIESE

⊱ *Apulian Green Beans in Tomato Sauce* ⊰

This simple green bean dish from Apulia yields excellent results with minimal fuss. It's a great weeknight dish, especially because it can be served cold (many would claim it's better chilled) and therefore made in advance. Italian vegetables are often cooked a bit longer than some people are used to, and this dish will help you understand why. Put aside any idea of crisp, crunchy green beans, and you'll be pleasantly surprised at how deliciously creamy they can become.

DURATION: 1 hour, largely unattended

YIELD: 3 or 4 servings

Salt

¼ cup (60 g) extra-virgin olive oil

1 clove garlic, peeled

1 dried or fresh chili pepper, chopped (optional)

About 20 ounces (570 g) cherry tomatoes (see Note), cut in half

1 pound (450 g) green beans, cleaned and trimmed

About 5 fresh basil leaves, torn

1. Put a large pot of water on to boil and salt it generously. While the water comes to a boil, begin cooking the tomato sauce.

2. In a large pan, heat the olive oil, garlic clove, and chili pepper over medium heat. When the garlic starts to sizzle, add the tomatoes and cook, stirring occasionally, until they soften and release their juices. Season with salt, then reduce the heat to medium-low and let gently simmer while you cook the green beans.

3. Add the green beans to the boiling water and cook for 15 minutes.

4. Transfer the beans to the tomato sauce with a slotted spoon. Stir everything together, along with a ladle of the boiling water, and bring to a simmer.

5. Let cook for another 20 to 25 minutes, until the green beans are very tender and the sauce has thickened. If the sauce thickens too much, add more water. Season with salt again as the dish nears completion. Stir in the basil at the end.

6. Serve warm or at room temperature.

NOTE *You can use chopped Roma or plum tomatoes, but cherry tomatoes pack a more flavorful punch.*

FAGIOLI ALLA TOSCANA

⤙ Tuscan Cannellini Beans ⤚

On our first trip to Tuscany together we tried a wealth of incredible food, ranging from tagliatelle with wild boar to the famous Fiorentina steak. Out of all the delicious dishes we sampled, the one we remember the most was a simple plate of cannellini beans, seasoned with salt, olive oil and black pepper. That's it. As with all simple dishes, the quality of the ingredients makes all the difference. Tuscan olive oil is spicy and flavorful, so try to find some that has a little kick. This is a dish that's worth bringing out the good stuff for.

DURATION: 2 hours, largely unattended

YIELD: 4 servings

14 ounces (400 g) dried cannellini beans (see Note)

Salt

1 clove garlic, peeled (optional)

Extra-virgin olive oil

Freshly ground black pepper

1. Place the beans in a medium pot (preferably terra-cotta) and fill with enough water to submerge them. Bring to a gentle simmer, partially covered. Stir the beans occasionally as they cook by gently swirling the pot around. Avoid using a spoon, as you risk breaking the beans, particularly in the later stages of cooking. Keep a kettle of warm water nearby and add more water as necessary to keep the beans slightly submerged. Cook until the beans are soft and tender but not mushy or dissolved, about 2 hours. When they are 5 to 10 minutes away from being done, generously season them with salt and add the garlic clove. Swirl to mix the seasoning in.

2. Transfer the beans to a serving plate with a slotted spoon, drizzle with plenty of olive oil, and sprinkle with pepper.

NOTE *High-quality beans will cook evenly and the skins will resist splitting. Great Northern beans are a close alternative that work well and are more widely available in North America. We usually opt for them unless we happen to have a very good cannellini source. We never soak beans in advance, although you can if you wish to shorten the cooking time. It's very easy to scale up the amount of beans too.*

INSALATA PANTESCA

✦⊱ *Sicilian Potato Salad* ⊰✦

This Sicilian potato salad is a far cry from the mayonnaise-laden version most of us are familiar with. It's light, fresh, and tangy—perfect for a hot summer day. If you're not a big fan of mayo, this is definitely a potato salad to try. It's best served the next day, after a night in the fridge.

DURATION: 1 hour, largely unattended

YIELD: 4 to 6 servings

2 pounds (900 g) russet potatoes, skins on

1 red onion, thinly sliced

White wine vinegar

12 ounces (340 g) cherry tomatoes, cut in half

20 to 30 pitted Kalamata olives, cut in half

1½ tablespoons (18 g) capers

Salt and freshly ground black pepper

Dried oregano

Extra-virgin olive oil

1. Place the potatoes in a large pot of water. Bring the water to a boil and cook the potatoes for 30 to 45 minutes, depending on their size, until you can insert a sharp paring knife into the center; they should be a little firmer than if you were planning to mash them.

2. While the potatoes are boiling, place the onion in a medium bowl and fill with vinegar until the slices are submerged. Let marinate while the potatoes cook.

3. Drain the potatoes and let cool to the touch.

4. Drain the onion and add it to a large serving bowl. Add the tomatoes, olives, and capers to the bowl and mix everything together.

5. Peel the cooled potatoes with a paring knife and cut into roughly 1½-inch (4 cm) chunks. Season with salt, pepper, and oregano, then generously drizzle with olive oil and mix well. (If you plan to serve it the next day, we recommend waiting to season it with salt until the day you serve it.)

6. Serve at room temperature.

CICORIA RIPASSATA

⇥ Stir-Fried Chicory with Garlic & Peperoncino ⇤

This central Italian side dish is a classic sight on menus in Rome and a go-to for us when dining out in the Eternal City. If you don't have access to chicory, you can use dandelion greens, although many will find the latter to be too bitter to eat alone (we love it, for the record). But don't worry; there are many ways to eat this dish. Try serving it in a sandwich (especially with sausages), on a bruschetta, or stuffed into focaccia.

DURATION: 30 minutes

YIELD: 4 servings

Salt

1 pound (450 g) chicory or dandelion greens

3 tablespoons (45 ml) extra-virgin olive oil

1 clove garlic, peeled

1 fresh or dried chili pepper, whole (less spicy) or chopped (spicier)

1. Bring a large pot of water to a boil and salt it generously. Add the chicory and boil for 5 minutes.

2. Shortly before the greens are done, heat the olive oil, garlic, and chili pepper in a large pan over medium heat.

3. Transfer the boiled chicory to the pan with tongs and cook, stirring occasionally, for 10 minutes, or until the liquid has thickened.

4. Serve hot.

INSALATA DI POMODORO

↦ Tomato Salad ↤

Nothing could be less Italian than the sugary, over-seasoned bottles of "Italian seasoning" that plague so many grocery-store condiment sections. Real Italian salads are very simple and rely on the natural flavors of good ingredients. If you take the time to find high-quality tomatoes that are in season, you don't need to douse them in sugar syrup for a delicious dish. This type of tomato salad can be found throughout Italy, but we can't help adding the Calabrian touch of oregano and chili pepper. Feel free to skip the pepper if you're sensitive to spiciness.

DURATION: 5 minutes

YIELD: 4 to 6 servings

3 large heirloom tomatoes, cut into 1-inch (2.5 cm) chunks or wedges

1 sweet onion, thinly sliced

1 fresh chili pepper, sliced

6 to 8 fresh basil leaves, torn

6 tablespoons (90 ml) extra-virgin olive oil

Dried oregano

Salt

1. In a medium bowl, thoroughly mix the tomatoes, onion, chili pepper, basil, and olive oil. Season with oregano.

2. Right before serving, season the salad with salt. (While you can make the salad in advance, don't salt the tomatoes until serving time, as the salt will cause them to drain their juices.)

3. Serve immediately.

INSALATA DI FINOCCHI, ARANCE E OLIVE NERE

⇥ *Fennel, Orange & Olive Salad* ⇤

The Sicilian tendency to mix sweet and savory extends even to their salads. Fennel, with its slightly sweet aftertaste, is the perfect base for ripe oranges and salty black olives. For the best results, thinly slice the fennel with a mandoline. If you can't find high-quality black olives, try substituting them with Kalamata olives, which are widely available and have much better flavor than canned black olives.

DURATION: 10 minutes

YIELD: 4 servings

1 large fennel bulb, fronds trimmed and thinly sliced

2 oranges, peeled and sliced

½ large sweet onion, sliced (optional)

About 20 pitted black olives

6 tablespoons (90 ml) extra-virgin olive oil

Salt and freshly ground black pepper

1. In a large bowl, thoroughly mix the fennel, oranges, onion (if using), olives, and olive oil. Season the salad with salt and pepper.

2. Serve cold.

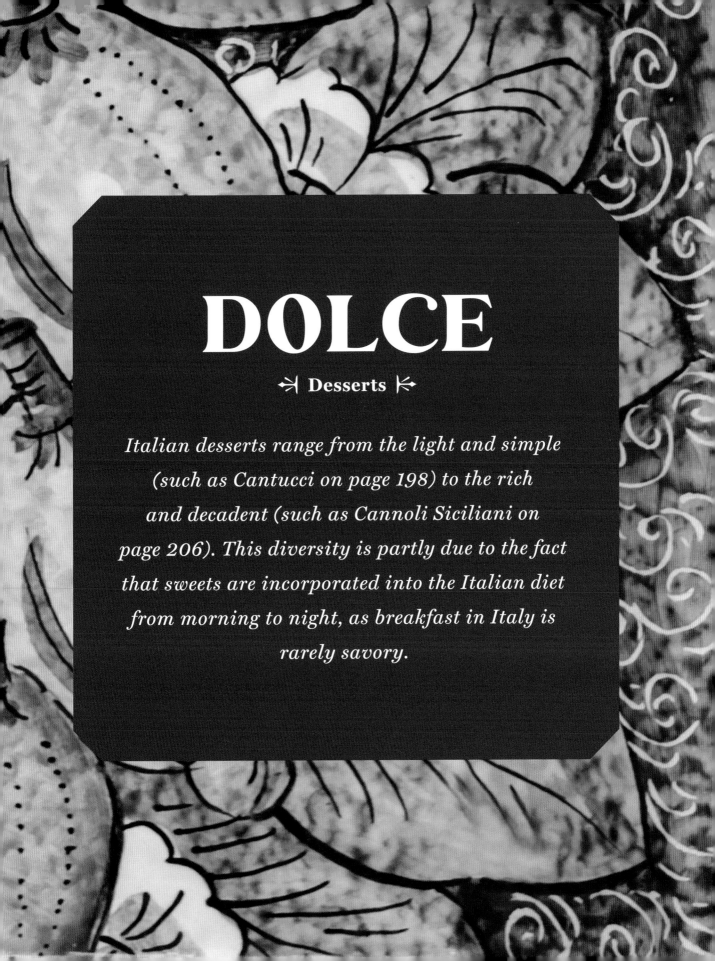

DOLCE

⊁ Desserts ⊱

Italian desserts range from the light and simple (such as Cantucci on page 198) to the rich and decadent (such as Cannoli Siciliani on page 206). This diversity is partly due to the fact that sweets are incorporated into the Italian diet from morning to night, as breakfast in Italy is rarely savory.

PASTE DI MANDORLA

⤙ *Sicilian Almond Cookies* ⤚

We've never introduced these unassuming little cookies to someone without getting the same shocked reaction. No one can believe how good they are until they taste them. These Sicilian almond cookies are incredibly simple and easy to make, and they have an extraordinary flavor and irresistibly gooey texture. They are traditionally topped with candied cherries, almonds, or sometimes even coffee beans.

DURATION: 1 hour
YIELD: 20 to 25 cookies

4½ tablespoons (70 g) egg whites (from 2 or 3 eggs)

1 teaspoon (5 ml) almond extract

2½ cups (250 g) almond flour

1½ cups (180 g) powdered sugar

Granulated sugar, for dusting

Candied cherries and/or whole almonds, for topping

1. In a large bowl, whisk the egg whites with a fork for a few minutes until they become slightly foamy. Add the almond extract, almond flour, and powdered sugar and mix the ingredients by hand. A dough will quickly form; shape this into a large ball, wrap in plastic wrap, and freeze it for 10 minutes.

2. Meanwhile, preheat the oven to 340°F (170°C). Line a large baking sheet with parchment paper.

3. Tear off chunks of the chilled dough and roll them into balls about 2 inches (5 cm) in diameter. Toss them in granulated sugar, press a shallow hole in the top with your finger, and place a candied cherry or almond into the depression.

4. Bake for 15 to 17 minutes, until the bottoms of the cookies are golden. Let cool completely before eating.

CANTUCCI

⊰ *Tuscan Biscotti Cookies* ⊱

When most people imagine "biscotti," they're usually picturing cantucci, which are simply one type of biscotto. These Tuscan cookies are easier to make than you might think and make a great gift, in no small part due to their relatively long shelf life. Traditionally they're served with some vin santo (sweet wine), in which the biscotti are dipped.

DURATION: 2 hours

YIELD: 25 biscotti

1 large egg

½ cup (125 g) granulated sugar

6 tablespoons (75 g) lard

½ teaspoon (2.5 ml) rose water (optional)

½ teaspoon (1.5 g) ground cinnamon (optional)

1 teaspoon (2.5 g) baking powder

2 cups (250 g) all-purpose flour

6 ounces (170 g) almonds, roughly chopped

1. Preheat the oven to 355°F (180°C). Line a baking sheet with parchment paper.

2. In a large bowl, combine the egg and sugar. Beat them with a hand mixer until white and creamy. Add the lard and continue to beat until it is well incorporated. Using a spatula, stir in the rose water (if using) and cinnamon (if using).

3. In a medium bowl, thoroughly mix the baking powder and flour. Gradually add the flour mixture to the egg mixture, folding it in with a spatula. When the dough thickens enough to handle, start mixing and kneading by hand.

4. When all the flour is well incorporated, transfer the dough to a clean work surface. Press it into a flat pancake shape, then spread a handful of chopped almonds on top. Fold and knead the almonds into the dough, then repeat until all the almonds are evenly mixed in.

5. Cut the dough into 2 equal portions. Roll each portion into a cylinder beneath your palms, about 3 inches (7.5 cm) in diameter. Take care to ensure that the width is even and the dough does not have large gaps or cracks. Place the cylinders 2 inches (5 cm) apart on the prepared baking sheet and gently press them to flatten them slightly.

6. Bake for 20 to 25 minutes, until lightly browned on top. Remove from the oven (leave the oven on) and let the half-cooked dough cool for 10 minutes, then carefully transfer to a cutting board.

7. Cut each dough portion widthwise into straight, 1-inch (2.5 cm) slices. Turn the slices onto their sides and arrange them on the prepared baking sheet. (It's okay to crowd them in, if necessary; they won't expand at all when cooked.)

8. Bake the biscotti for an additional 10 minutes. Allow the cookies to cool completely before serving. Store in a plastic bag or an airtight container at room temperature for up to 2 weeks.

CROSTATA DI MARMELLATA

→| Fruit Jam Tart |←

"Crostata" is a very general term for a broad category of Italian tarts. The pasta frolla dough, which is similar to a piecrust, is usually the same, but the filling can consist of ricotta, jam, or a combination of both. We've chosen to share a marmalade crostata recipe, which is always fun to make because you can use any fruit you like. A crostata is thinner than a pie, but usually a little too thick for a traditional tart tin. We therefore recommend making it in a shallow pie dish; just be aware that it won't fill the dish to the rim.

DURATION: 1½ hours

YIELD: One 9-inch (23 cm) tart

2½ cups (300 g) all-purpose flour, plus more for dusting

¾ cup (100 g) powdered sugar, plus more for dusting

10 tablespoons (150 g) cold unsalted butter, cut into small chunks, plus more for greasing

1 large egg, at room temperature

Grated zest of 1 lemon

24 ounces (680 g) fruit jam or marmalade

1. In a large bowl, combine the flour, powdered sugar, butter, egg, and lemon zest. Knead everything together by hand until an even dough forms. Shape the dough into a ball, wrap it in plastic wrap, and refrigerate for 30 minutes.

2. Preheat the oven to 355°F (180°C). Grease a 9-inch (23 cm) pie dish with butter. Dust the dish with flour to lightly coat and discard the excess.

3. Remove the dough from the fridge and cut off about two-thirds. Keep the remaining one-third wrapped in the fridge. Roll out the dough with a rolling pin on a floured work surface until it is large enough to fill the pie dish up to the rim. Dust the dough lightly with flour if it sticks to the rolling pin. Drape the dough into the dish and gently press it down to fill all the bottom corners.

4. Spread the jam evenly into the tart crust. Roll out the remaining dough to the same thickness as the bottom crust and cut it into 6 long strips, each ½ inch (13 mm) wide. Lay 3 strips parallel to each other on top of the tart, then arrange the remaining 3 strips on top in the opposite direction. (Crostate rarely feature a lattice pattern, but feel free to make one if you like.)

5. Bake for 25 to 30 minutes, until the top crust is golden. Let the crostata cool to room temperature.

6. Top with a dusting of powdered sugar before slicing and serving.

ZUPPA INGLESE

⤙ *Trifle with Sponge Cake, Custard & Alchermes Liqueur* ⤚

Zuppa Inglese, or "English soup," probably originated as an attempt to replicate a British trifle. The dessert can be thought of as a fruitier tiramisù, although zuppa Inglese predates the latter. Contrary to the implications of the name, the key to making a great zuppa Inglese is to avoid it becoming too soupy, which is easily done by drizzling the sponge cake with a minimal amount of liqueur instead of dipping it—a common mistake. For the real deal, you'll need to find Alchermes (a red liqueur flavored with cinnamon, cloves, and nutmeg). In a pinch, feel free to substitute with a different liqueur; you'll still have a delicious dessert. Zuppa Inglese, like tiramisù, is best made a day in advance. For even better results, make the custard and sponge cake two days prior. Let the custards chill in the fridge and keep the sponge cake (once cool) wrapped in plastic wrap.

DURATION: 5 hours, largely unattended (the sponge cake and custards are best made 2 days in advance and the completed dessert is best made 1 day in advance)

YIELD: One 2-quart (2 L) zuppa Inglese; 4 to 6 servings

Sponge Cake

5 large eggs

¾ cup (150 g) granulated sugar

Grated zest of 1 lemon

1⅓ cups (160 g) all-purpose flour

Alchermes liqueur, for drizzling

Custards

4¼ cups (1 L) whole milk

1 teaspoon (5 ml) vanilla extract

8 large egg yolks

¾ cup (150 g) granulated sugar

½ cup (60 g) all-purpose flour

⅔ cup (50 g) unsweetened dark cocoa powder, plus more for dusting

1. To make the sponge cake: Preheat the oven to 350°F (175°C). Line a 9-inch (23 cm) round cake pan with parchment paper, leaving some overhang so that you can easily remove the cake from the pan later.

2. In a large bowl, beat the eggs, sugar, and lemon zest with a hand mixer for 20 minutes. (You might be tempted to stop mixing when the eggs become fluffy, but the 20-minute timing is important for incorporating enough air into the eggs.)

3. Adding a little bit at a time, sift the 1⅓ cups (160 g) flour into the eggs with a fine-mesh sieve, and gently fold it in with a spatula. Pour the sponge cake into the prepared cake pan.

4. Bake for 30 to 35 minutes, until golden on top. Pull out the cake from the pan using the parchment paper and let cool to room temperature on a wire rack. For the best results, wrap the cooled cake in plastic wrap and let rest at room temperature overnight.

5. While the sponge cake bakes, prepare the custards: In a medium pot, warm the milk and vanilla over low heat; the milk should not come to a boil but just be warm to the touch. Meanwhile, mix together the egg yolks and sugar in a large bowl until incorporated, then thoroughly mix in the ½ cup (60 g) flour.

continued on following page >>

6. When the milk is warm, add 2 or 3 ladlefuls of it to the egg yolks and mix until the yolks and milk are well incorporated. Pour the yolk mixture into the milk pot and cook at a very low temperature, stirring constantly, until the milk has thickened into a runny custard, about 15 minutes.

7. Evenly divide the custard between two large bowls. Cover one with plastic wrap so that the plastic is in contact with the surface to prevent a skin from developing. Whisk the cocoa powder into the other bowl of custard until there are no clumps of powder. Cover this bowl in plastic wrap in the same manner. Let the custards cool to room temperature, then chill in the refrigerator for at least 1 hour, or preferably overnight.

8. Cut the sponge cake into slices, about ⅓ inch (8 mm) thick. Arrange a single layer of cake slices on the bottom of a 2-quart (2 L) baking dish. Cut smaller pieces as necessary to fill any gaps. Using a spoon, drizzle just enough Alchermes over the sponge cake to lightly saturate it. (Don't worry if there's still some white cake showing in spots; it's better to use too little than too much.) Cover the sponge cake with an even layer of plain custard, spread evenly from edge to edge.

9. Create a second layer of cake slices and drizzle with more Alchermes. Cover this with a layer of cocoa custard. Make a third cake layer, drizzled with Alchermes and top with a final layer of custard; you can use only the white custard, but we like covering one-half with white and the other half with cocoa.

10. Cover the zuppa Inglese with plastic wrap and let chill in the refrigerator overnight for the best results.

11. Right before serving, dust the top evenly with cocoa powder.

STRUFFOLI

⇥ Fried Dough Balls Glazed in Honey ⇤

If you let your eyes wander across an Italian Christmas table set for dessert, you'll have a lot to look at, but you will inevitably find yourself fixated on the struffoli. This dessert is made up of a ton of little fried dough balls, glazed together with honey and decorated with sprinkles and candied cherries. Everyone reaches over, pulls off a ball or two, and snacks away on this addicting treat all night. Honey is a natural preservative, which explains the origins of this odd dish. Once made, it keeps at room temperature for weeks. Christmas lasts a long time in Italy, so this was a way to have a sweet treat around that lasted for the duration of the feasting period.

DURATION: 3 hours, largely unattended

YIELD: 1 platter of struffoli (enough to serve a large gathering or an addicted diner)

3⅓ cups (400 g) all-purpose flour, plus more for dusting

3 large eggs

1 large egg yolk

3½ tablespoons (45 g) sugar

4½ tablespoons (65 g) lard

Grated zest of 1 lemon

Pinch of salt

4 teaspoons (20 ml) limoncello (you can use rum), divided

Peanut oil (or other neutral oil), for frying

½ cup (120 ml) honey

Multicolored sprinkles, for decorating

Candied cherries, for decorating

1. Pour the flour into a pile on a large, clean work surface. Hollow out the center with your hand. Into the hollow, add the eggs, egg yolk, sugar, lard, lemon zest, salt, and 3 teaspoons (15 ml) of the limoncello.

2. Using your hand, begin mixing the ingredients together while incorporating the surrounding flour into a rough dough. Knead the dough until it is very smooth and uniform. Wrap it in plastic and let it rest at room temperature for 2 hours.

3. Dust a large baking sheet or cutting board with flour. Cut a golf ball-size chunk of dough from the main ball and roll it under your palms into a long snake, about 1 finger in width. Slice this strand into small pieces, about a finger's width in length. Place these onto the floured baking sheet and repeat until you have used up all the dough.

4. Fill a large, deep pan with about 2 inches (5 cm) of oil and heat to frying temperature (see How to Fry at Home on page 34). Place 2 or 3 handfuls of dough balls into a fine-mesh strainer, gently shake them to remove any excess flour, and carefully pour them into the oil. Fry, stirring occasionally, until golden. Remove them with a slotted spoon to a paper towel–lined plate to drain. Repeat to fry the remaining dough balls.

continued on following page >>

5. Add the honey and remaining 1 teaspoon (5 ml) limoncello to a large nonstick pan over medium-low heat. As soon as the honey melts and starts to bubble, pour all the fried dough balls into the pan. Stirring and turning constantly with a spatula, cook the struffoli until all the honey has been absorbed by the dough. Turn off the heat and let cool for 1 to 2 minutes before plating.

6. Arrange the struffoli as desired. The simplest way to plate them is in a large pile on a serving platter. If you are feeling fancy, you can also heap them around a cup or jar that can be removed later, to create a ring shape.

7. While the honey is still warm, sprinkle the dessert with sprinkles. If you made a ring shape, wait until the honey has cooled but not completely hardened before carefully removing the center cup.

8. Top the dish with a few well-placed candied cherries. Allow the honey to cool and harden completely before serving.

CANNOLI SICILIANI

✒ *Fried Shells Stuffed with Sweet Ricotta* ✒

There are a few different styles of cannoli in Sicily, most notably those of Messina and Palermo. This recipe is in the latter style, which can most readily be identified by a darker shell made with some added cocoa powder. To make your own cannoli shells, you'll need a pasta machine and some 5-inch (12.5 cm) cannoli molds. What truly makes Sicilian cannoli stand out is the use of sheep's and/or goat's milk ricotta, which have a cheesier bite than cow's milk ricotta. Since most people don't have access to real ricotta di pecora (or even real ricotta at all, a certainty if you live in the United States), use the best you can find. At the very least, you can rest assured that your cannoli will be leagues better than the whipped cream–filled knockoffs that are all too common.

DURATION: 2 hours, plus some prep done 2 days in advance

YIELD: 15 to 20 cannoli

---

24 ounces (680 g) ricotta

Powdered sugar

1 cup (120 g) all-purpose flour, plus more for dusting

3 teaspoons (12 g) granulated sugar

½ tablespoon (2.5 g) unsweetened cocoa powder

½ teaspoon (2.5 g) salt

1 tablespoon (15 g) lard

2 tablespoons (30 ml) Marsala wine

1 teaspoon (5 ml) white vinegar

1 large egg

Sunflower or peanut oil, for frying

About 1 cup (240 g) mini chocolate chips, or to taste (optional)

Crushed pistachios, candied orange peel, and/or candied cherries for topping (optional)

1. Two days before you plan on filling your cannoli shells, place the ricotta into a fine-mesh strainer over a bowl. Cover with plastic wrap and let it drain overnight in the refrigerator. Discard the drained water.

2. The next day, mix the ricotta with powdered sugar to taste. Place it back into the mesh strainer and drain in the refrigerator overnight again.

3. The following day, combine the flour, granulated sugar, cocoa powder, salt, lard, Marsala wine, and vinegar in a large bowl. Whisk the egg separately until beaten, then add 3½ teaspoons (17 ml) of it into the mixing bowl. (Reserve the remaining egg for assembling the shells.)

4. Mix the ingredients by hand until they begin to form into a rough dough. (Don't be surprised if it seems quite dry at first; just keep working it and the dough will come together.) Transfer the dough to a clean work surface and knead it for about 10 minutes, or until it is evenly mixed. Wrap the dough in plastic wrap and refrigerate it for 1 hour.

5. Lightly dust the chilled dough with flour, flatten it under your palm, and roll it out using a pasta machine. Start with the largest thickness setting (usually #0 or #1), then fold the dough sheet in half lengthwise and roll it again. (Don't worry if the dough breaks at first; just keep folding and rolling.) Repeat the folding process about 5 to 8 times; this will trap air in the dough and create the classic cannoli shell bubbles when fried. If the dough sticks to the machine, lightly dust it with more flour.

6. Once you have repeated the folding several times, gradually roll the dough thinner by reducing the thickness setting of the machine by one click after each pass; the desired thickness is 1.5 to 2 mm (#5 or #6 on a standard Marcato Atlas 150 pasta machine). Lightly dust the dough with flour as necessary. If the sheet of dough becomes too long to comfortably handle, cut it in half and roll a portion at a time.

7. With a knife, cut the dough into perfect squares, about 4 × 4 inches (10 × 10 cm). Wrap each square diagonally around a cannoli mold and "glue" the joined corners together with a dab of the reserved whisked egg. Do not wrap them too tight, though; you want to leave a tiny bit of space around the mold so that the shell has some room to expand.

8. Fill a large, deep pan with about 2 inches (5 cm) of oil and heat to frying temperature. In this case, we recommend using a thermometer and keeping the oil at around 355°F (180°C). Working in batches, carefully drop the cannoli shells, still on the molds, into the oil and fry, turning gently with tongs, until golden on all sides, 2 minutes at the most but usually 1 minute or less. Remove to a paper towel–lined plate to drain and cool. When the shells are cool enough to handle, gently slide them off the molds. The shells are ready to fill once they have cooled completely.

9. Press the drained ricotta through a fine-mesh sieve into a large bowl using a spatula. You will likely need to do so in batches, depending on the size of your sieve. This process makes the ricotta much smoother, and the results are better the more you do it, so feel free to repeat 2 or 3 times.

10. Mix the sweetened ricotta with mini chocolate chips (if using). Right before serving, use a spoon to press the filling into each end of a cannolo shell, being sure to fill it completely.

11. If using any of the toppings, either dip the ends in crushed pistachio nuts or garnish them with a slice of candied orange peel or a candied cherry. Top the cannoli with a dusting of powdered sugar.

TIRAMISÙ

→ Ladyfinger Layer Cake with Coffee & Mascarpone Custard ←

Tiramisù should never be ordered in a restaurant, even in Italy. Preparing the mascarpone cream is too costly for chefs, so they inevitably use whipped cream, which is an unacceptable substitution. The only way to eat the real thing is to make it at home. Traditionally, this dessert is made with raw eggs. We still make ours that way (and always will), but we've chosen to share a reassuring method here that safely pasteurizes the eggs without sacrificing flavor. It requires a little bit more work and an instant-read thermometer. If you wish to go traditional, use all the same ingredient amounts but skip the simple-syrup preparation. Beat all the sugar into the egg yolks until very smooth and almost white, then mix in the mascarpone. Set this aside, clean and dry your mixer very well, then beat the egg whites. Gently fold the egg whites into the yolk mixture a little bit at a time.

DURATION: 1 to 1½ hours (best made a day in advance)

YIELD: One 2-quart (2 L) tiramisù (we recommend an 8 × 8-inch, or 20 × 20 cm) dish to get maximum height, but a rectangular dish works as well); 8 to 10 servings

---

6 large eggs

¾ cup (150 g) granulated sugar, divided

16 ounces (450 g) mascarpone cheese

Pinch of salt

3 cups (700 ml) espresso coffee diluted with 1 cup (240 ml) water

16 ounces (450 g) savoiardi ("ladyfinger") biscuits (see Note on page 210)

Unsweetened cocoa powder, for topping

1. Separate the egg yolks and whites, placing the yolks in one large bowl and the whites in another.

2. Add ¼ cup (50 g) of the sugar to the egg yolks and beat with a hand mixer until the eggs begin to foam. Set it aside while you prepare a simple syrup.

3. In a small saucepan, combine ¼ cup (50 g) of the sugar with 5 teaspoons (25 ml) of water. Heat over medium heat, stirring occasionally, while monitoring the temperature with an instant-read thermometer until the syrup reaches 250°F (121°C).

4. Pour the simple syrup into the egg yolks, beating with the hand mixer until the yolks are nearly white and the sugar has dissolved completely. Add the mascarpone and thoroughly mix it in. Wash and dry the hand mixer.

5. Add the salt to the egg whites and beat with the clean hand mixer until the egg whites are fluffy but not stiff.

6. Make a second simple syrup with the remaining ¼ cup (50 g) sugar and 5 teaspoons of water. Heat as in step 3 over medium heat, stirring occasionally, to 250°F (121°C). Add this syrup to the egg whites, beating with the hand mixer until the bowl can be held upside down without the egg whites spilling.

continued on following page >>

7. Adding a little bit at a time, mix the egg whites into the yolk-mascarpone mixture, gently folding them in with a spatula. (Try to avoid vigorous stirring, as this will cause the egg whites to lose volume.) Continue to add and fold until all the egg whites are evenly mixed in.

8. Pour the diluted coffee into a shallow bowl or dish. Quickly dip a savoiardi biscuit in the coffee, shake off the excess, and place it in the bottom of a 2-quart (2 L) dish. Continue to arrange coffee-dipped biscuits in a tight layer that covers the bottom of the dish completely. There should be no gaps, so cut the savoiardi into smaller pieces as necessary to fill in holes.

9. Spread a layer of egg-mascarpone "cream" over all the biscuits; the layer should not be too thick but just enough to cover the savoiardi completely and up to the edges of the dish. Repeat with layers of savoiardi topped with cream until you have run out of space or biscuits. Depending on the shape of your dish, you should end up with 3 or 4 layers. Finish with a final layer of cream.

10. A tiramisù is best served the next day after being refrigerated overnight. If you cannot wait 24 hours, at least try to give it a few hours to chill so that the coffee can properly disperse into and among the savoiardi.

11. Dust the tiramisù with cocoa powder right before cutting and serving.

NOTE *A lot of recipes outside of Italy include instructions for making homemade ladyfinger biscuits. While this sounds great in theory, it makes Italians scratch their heads. It's akin to making homemade crackers for a graham cracker crust. We recommend just buying a package of savoiardi cookies, which are widely available these days.*

TORTA DELLA NONNA

⤚| *Custard Pie with Pine Nuts* |⤙

Torta della nonna, or "grandmother's cake," is so-called because of its status as *the* go-to, home-cooked dessert that every Italian's nonna makes. It's a simple, custard-filled pie that's sure to keep the kids and grandkids coming back for another slice.

DURATION: 4 to 5 hours, largely unattended

YIELD: One 9-inch (23 cm) pie

Custard

1 lemon

4¼ cups (1 L) whole milk

6 large egg yolks

1 cup (200 g) granulated sugar

¾ cup (100 g) cornstarch

Piecrust

2½ cups (300 g) all-purpose flour, plus more for dusting

10 tablespoons (150 g) cold unsalted butter, cut into chunks

2 large eggs, at room temperature, divided

¾ cup (100 g) powdered sugar, plus more for topping

½ teaspoon (2.5 ml) vanilla extract

3 tablespoons pine nuts, or to taste, for topping

1. To make the custard: Carefully shave off the yellow peel (avoid the white pith) of the lemon with a sharp paring knife. Try to shave it off in long pieces, as this will make it easier to remove from the custard later.

2. In a medium saucepan, warm the milk and lemon peel over low heat.

3. Meanwhile, whisk together the egg yolks and granulated sugar in a large bowl until the sugar completely dissolves. Thoroughly mix the cornstarch into the egg yolks.

4. Gradually pour the warm milk and lemon peel into the bowl with the egg yolks while whisking. After the milk is incorporated, transfer the mixture back into the saucepan and cook over low heat, stirring constantly, until the custard thickens, 20 to 30 minutes. Pick out and discard the lemon peel.

5. Transfer the custard to a large bowl and cover with plastic wrap so that the plastic is in contact with the surface to prevent a skin from developing. Let cool to room temperature, then refrigerate for 1 hour.

6. Meanwhile, make the piecrust: In a large bowl, combine the flour, butter, 1 egg, powdered sugar, and vanilla. Knead by hand until an even dough forms. Shape the dough into a ball, wrap in plastic wrap, and refrigerate for 1 hour.

7. Preheat the oven to 350°F (175°C).

continued on following page >>

8. Remove the dough from the fridge and cut off about two-thirds. Keep the remaining one-third wrapped in the fridge.

9. On a lightly floured work surface, roll out the dough with a rolling pin until it is large enough to fill a 9-inch (23 cm) pie dish with some overhang. If the dough sticks to the rolling pin, dust it with flour. Drape the dough into the pie dish and gently press it down to fill the bottom corners. (One trick to help you move the dough is to gently roll it up on the rolling pin, then unroll it on top of the pie dish.)

10. Fill the piecrust with the chilled custard. Roll out the remaining dough until it is large enough to cover the surface of the pie. Drape it on top, trim off the overhang, and fold and press the edges inward to seal the pie.

11. Whisk the remaining egg and brush the top piecrust with it. Rinse the pine nuts (being wet will prevent burning) and evenly sprinkle them over the crust.

12. Bake for 45 to 50 minutes, until the crust is golden. Let the pie cool completely.

13. Dust with powdered sugar, slice, and serve.

PASTIERA NAPOLETANA

⊶| *Neapolitan Easter Pie* |↞

This pie is Eva's favorite dessert of all time. She counts down the days until Easter just for this treat. The filling is made from ricotta, eggs, and cooked wheat and is so delicious, you'll find yourself wanting to make it as a standalone custard. The secret behind a real pastiera is fior d'arancia, a liquid orange blossom essence that comes in little vials in Italy. Finding it can be tricky, but many Italian markets and online vendors sell it. We wish we could offer a good substitute, but there isn't one. You can use a teaspoon of orange extract if need be, but what you end up with won't be a pastiera. Since you'll probably need to search out a specialty market for cooked wheat (jarred precooked wheat berries) anyway, try to find the real deal. This recipe is worth the search. The ingredients don't easily divide, and cooked wheat grain generally comes in a 500-gram jar that's enough for two pies anyway, so the recipe is for two pastiere. Trust us, you won't complain about having an extra one.

DURATION: 2 to 3 hours, plus 24 hours cooling and resting

YIELD: Two 9-inch (23 cm) pies

Piecrusts

4⅛ cups (500 g) all-purpose flour, plus more for dusting

14 tablespoons (200 g) unsalted butter, at room temperature and cut into small chunks, plus more for greasing

⅔ cup (150 g) granulated sugar

3 large eggs

1 large egg yolk

Pinch of grated orange zest

Powdered sugar, for topping

1. To make the piecrusts: In a large bowl, combine the flour, 14 tablespoons (200 g) butter, ⅔ cup (150 g) granulated sugar, 3 eggs, 1 egg yolk, and orange zest. Quickly mix by hand until a rough dough forms.

2. Transfer the dough to a flat work surface and knead it until it is smooth and uniform. (It's important to work quickly so that the butter doesn't completely melt.) Form the dough into 2 equal balls, wrap them in plastic, and let chill in the refrigerator for at least 30 minutes.

3. Meanwhile, make the filling: In a large saucepan, combine the cooked wheat, milk, and 1 tablespoon (15 g) butter. Heat over medium-low heat, stirring with a whisk, until the mixture thickens; it should be a little bit thinner than a custard. Let cool completely.

4. As the milk cools, press the ricotta through a fine-mesh sieve with a spatula; this will help make it smooth and creamy. Mix the ricotta, 2¼ cups (500 g) granulated sugar, 5 eggs, 3 egg yolks, vanilla, fior d'arancio, and candied citron into the milk mixture. Stir well.

Filling

17½ ounces (500 g) cooked wheat grain

1¼ cups (300 ml) whole milk

1 tablespoon (15 g) unsalted butter

24½ ounces (700 g) ricotta

2¼ cups (500 g) granulated sugar

5 large eggs

3 large egg yolks

½ teaspoon (2.5 ml) vanilla extract

2½ teaspoons (12 ml) fior d'arancio

5½ ounces (150 g) candied citron or orange peel, finely chopped

5. Preheat the oven to 395°F (200°C) and move a rack to the middle. Grease two 9-inch (23 cm) pie dishes with butter and dust them completely with flour. Dump out the excess flour.

6. Remove one of the dough portions from the refrigerator. Dust a large work surface lightly with flour and roll out the dough with a rolling pin until it is about ⅛ inch (3 mm) thick and large enough to cover a pie dish with plenty of overhang. Dust the dough with flour as needed to prevent sticking.

7. Drape the crust over your dish. Gently press it into the bottom corners for a nice fit. Trim the overhanging edges and save these scraps for later. Pour the filling into the piecrust until it is almost to the rim (leave a little room for the top crust). Roll out the dough trimmings to the same thickness as the bottom crust and cut them into long, 1-inch-wide (2.5 cm) strips. Lay these over the pie to make a checkerboard or lattice pattern. Trim off the edges of the strips. Repeat steps 6 and 7 with the remaining dough and filling to make the second pie.

8. Bake the pies on the middle rack for about 1 hour, or until browned on top. (Don't be alarmed if the pies rise quite a bit in the oven; they will settle flat as they cool.). Remove from the oven and let cool at room temperature for 1 day before eating.

9. Dust the pies with powdered sugar right before slicing and serving. Cover with plastic wrap and store in the refrigerator for 4 to 5 days.

TORTA DI MELE DI SANT'ORFEO

⇥ *Umbrian Apple Cake* ⇤

Most apple cakes are cakes flavored with apple. This version is almost entirely made of fruit, with just a small amount of cake batter to hold it together. The result is a cake that stays moist, is difficult to mess up, and is, in our opinion, much more delicious.

DURATION: 1½ hours

YIELD: One 9-inch (23 cm) cake

---

1 cup (120 g) raisins (see Note)

10½ tablespoons (150 g) unsalted butter, plus more for greasing the pan

½ cup (100 g) granulated sugar

½ cup (60 g) all-purpose flour, plus more for dusting

3 large eggs

5 medium apples, peeled, cored, and cut into 1-inch (2.5 cm) chunks

1 medium pear, peeled, cored, and cut into 1-inch (2.5 cm) chunks

1 teaspoon (2.5 g) ground cinnamon, or to taste

2 tablespoons (30 ml) whole milk

1 tablespoon (16 g) baking powder

1. Preheat the oven to 340°F (170°C). Place the raisins in a medium bowl and cover with water to soak while you prepare the batter.

2. Set up a bain-marie by filling a large saucepan with enough water so that a medium heat-resistant mixing bowl can nest inside with the bottom partially submerged in the liquid. Place the butter in the bowl, place the bain-marie over low heat, and melt the butter.

3. Once the butter has melted completely, gradually whisk in the sugar. Take the bowl out of the saucepan and gradually add the flour while whisking. Whisk in 1 egg at a time until each is fully incorporated.

4. Stir the apple and pear chunks into the batter. Drain the raisins, squeeze out the excess moisture, and pat them dry with a paper towel. Stir in the raisins and cinnamon.

5. In a small bowl, stir together the milk and baking powder until the baking powder dissolves (it will foam up quite a bit). Add this mixture to the batter and mix thoroughly.

6. Rub the bottom and sides of a 9-inch (23 cm) springform pan with butter, then dust it with flour and discard the excess. Pour the batter into the pan and bake for 1 hour, or until a knife inserted into the center comes out clean. Let the cake cool completely before removing the springform pan.

7. Slice and serve.

NOTE *If you're not a fan of raisins, you can easily substitute dried cranberries or chocolate chips.*

⊰ INDEX ⊱

⊰ ACKNOWLEDGMENTS ⊱

The idea behind this book began formulating almost as soon as we launched our YouTube channel. In those early days, we had little external support, and the project lay dormant on an indefinite back burner until several key people recently came together to finally make it happen. To them, we are grateful and would like to extend our thanks.

First and foremost, we would like to thank our manager, David Keller, and the team at Algebra Media for their assistance in growing and supporting our YouTube channel. If we hadn't made it this far as a channel, the book would never have been possible. Many thanks to Harper's father, Max Alexander, whose early editorial advice was invaluable. Our agent, Tim Moore, is responsible for rescuing this project from near abandonment, and for that, we owe him our gratitude. We would also like to thank Erin Canning and the team at Quarto for helping us put together a finished cookbook that far exceeds our early dreams and visions for what this project could be.

Above all, we would like to extend our deepest gratitude to the people of Italy. Generations of Italians developed these recipes over many centuries; we are merely compilers and interpreters. We hope that we have done justice to and served well the cuisine and culture of a people we love and to whom we are indebted.

⊰ ABOUT THE AUTHORS ⊱

Eva Santaguida left her home in Calabria, Italy, at a young age to pursue a career as an Italian language teacher. Her education and work took her to various parts of Italy, where she immersed herself in studying the diverse regional cuisines. After relocating to the United States with her American husband, Harper Alexander, Eva was surprised to find that the American interpretation of Italian food scarcely resembled the dishes she knew from home. Determined to share the authenticity and diversity of Italian cuisine, Eva and Harper launched the successful YouTube channel *Pasta Grammar*. On the channel, Eva combines her teaching expertise with her culinary passion to bring authentic Italian recipes to a global audience.

Harper Alexander was a cinematographer in Los Angeles before meeting his future wife, Eva Santaguida. A native of Calabria and a talented cook, Eva introduced Harper to the rich and varied world of Italian cuisine, transforming his views on food, culture, and nutrition. Inspired by his culinary journey, Harper decided to blend his filmmaking expertise with his passion for Italian food. Together with Eva, he cofounded *Pasta Grammar*, a YouTube channel dedicated to traditional Italian cooking. On the channel, Harper applies his visual storytelling skills to share and celebrate authentic Italian recipes with an international audience.